Gadgets,

Gimmicks

and

Grace

Gadgets,

Gimmicks

and

Grace

A Handbook on Multimedia
in Church and School

Edward N. McNulty

ABBEY PRESS • St. Meinrad, Indiana 47577

BV
1535
m3

Library of Congress Cataloging in Publication Data
McNulty, Edward N   1936-
    Gadgets, gimmicks, and grace.
    Bibliography: p.
    1.   Christian   education—Audio-visual   aids.
I.   Title.
BV1535.M3   268'.028   76-12094
ISBN 0-87029-060-6

To SANDRA,
whose faith and help made this book a reality

Contents

Preface

This book is designed for the person interested in media production in the church or school. Too many people have an unhealthy fear of the gadgets and gimmicks involved in media work. Hopefully the practical step by step suggestions will dispel the mystique that has grown up around media productions so that anyone who is willing to work hard can create an effective slide or multimedia show.

Gadgets, Gimmicks and Grace has grown out of the multimedia workshops which I have conducted. At the time I became active in this field there were no such works in print. In our impatience with publishers my wife and I produced this in mimeographed form. About 400 good folk, from pastors and Directors of Christian Education to youth, college and seminary professors, bought and used the work. Encouraged by their comments, I have added the chapter on filmmaking and updated the resource sections. Since this was first written four years ago two other books on the subject have appeared, but after looking them over I am convinced that *G G & G* is unique. The true media lover will want all three since each work brings a special insight to an exciting subject.

I have served in small churches and large ones but have always had to pay for my media work with my own funds—so the needs of the near-poverty church have been kept in mind. Productions ranging in cost from two or three dollars to a hundred are described; the sense of accomplishment growing out of successfully showing your first slide show is no less than that from a four-projector extravaganza. AV technical jargon has been kept to a minimum; the AV manuals contain enough of this. If I use myself as an example at times, it is to say to the reader, "Look, I've had no professional training in audio-visuals and have often had to scrounge around for equipment. If I can do it, so can you!"

Before the "nuts and bolts" of multimedia are probed, some of the theological ramifications of media and art are briefly explored in Chapter One. Some of you might be so eager "to get on with it" that you will want to skip this. This is fine for an initial reading, but before beginning a production, I urge you to go back and read the foundation chapter. You will find that the insights there will give you some handles that will be very useful as you plunge into media. These are not original with me but are gleaned from artists and theologians who are far more creative. They are "my" insights only in the sense that they have become a vital part of my life—of my way of seeing, of experiencing God and my world.

Of course, I have received much help along the way. Assistance from friends in regard to equipment, help from artists and thinkers, most of whom I have met only through their books and articles—such folk as Corita Kent, Harvey Cox, Roger Hazelton, Robert Short, Paul Simon, to name but a few. I acknowledge most of my debts in the Resource List at the end of this book.

I feel a special debt of gratitude to my friend Dennis Benson, whose enthusiasm for electronic media and the Gospel has inspired so many of us to plunge more deeply into media. Through his books, tapes, newsletters and workshops, Dennis has helped many of us discover new possibilities for ministry in and out of the church. Also, the youth of the churches I have served in West Virginia were willing guinea pigs for my first attempts at multimedia. Since then many members of the *Probe* Newsletter community have encouraged me through their use of my multimedia kits and their reports and criticisms of them. Most of all, as far as this volume is concerned, I am indebted to my wife Sandra, whose encouragement helped to begin it and who suggested that it be brought out in mimeographed form when no one else seemed interested.

The responses from so many readers, and now this Abbey Press edition, have justified her faith.

We offer this in fear and trembling to those in and outside of the church who are looking for new ways to express ancient truth. Nowhere is the claim made that multimedia will "save" the church or bring in hordes of new members. I do believe, however, that it is a valid and exciting tool when used with integrity (hence the addition of "Grace" to the book title). It can be a very frustrating form of communication at times, but in the end always fun. Through this book I hope to share some of the fun with you. May it contribute to your growing creativity as the Creator Spirit continues to move among us.

Pittsburgh, Pennsylvania
November, 1975

Visual

Parables

For Those "With Eyes That See"

This chapter could be summed up in one short imperative: Read the books listed in the section of the Bibliography called "Toward a Theology of Media." Why go on then? Why not get on with the nuts-and-bolts concerns, the "how" of multimedia? After all, as was stated in the Preface, many of you will skip this chapter in your impatience to get down to the "practical." However, sooner or later, if multimedia is going to be more than a faddish gimmick, you will have to wrestle with the "why" of multimedia. And this will lead you to some serious-playful grappling with the whole question of seeing and hearing—of how and why the Christian perceives God, himself and the swirling times. A tall order for one chapter—obviously we will only be able to offer some clues here and guide the reader to the works which are the source of these thoughts.

Multimedia demands a new way of seeing and hearing for both producer and audience. It is the result of projecting two or more images and sounds simultaneously; these may be slides, movie films, overhead transparencies or special lighting effects. The whole becomes greater than the sum of the parts in the consciousness of the viewer. He has to cope with the unexpected and the unaccustomed. Accustomed to handling one sequence of images at a time (in the same linear-type sequence in which he reads a book), he is unsettled by simultaneous projections. They create a mix in his mind. These are no longer isolated images but become related to each other. The secret of multimedia viewing (and producing) is to be able to see and appreciate that changing, shifting relationship.

For example: a sixty-second TV commercial depicts an unsure couple in a fancy restaurant gorging themselves so much that they need a leading stomach medicine for their "after-dinner drink." As you see and hear this, a series of slides are shown on both sides of the film. Pictures of people dieting opposite scenes of East Bengal refugees; ads for pet foods juxtaposed with pictures of people starving. Interwoven throughout both sets of slides are shots of a slim woman exercising "excess fat away" (one of America's major health problems!). Shown one at a time in linear sequence the pictures may be interesting, the film very amusing, but mixed together they emphasize the scandalous disparity between the "haves and the have-nots" in a forceful way.

Such a three-image mix (two sets of twenty slides plus the film) moves so fast that there is no time for the viewer to indulge in intellectualizing. He has time only to experience the images and the feelings which they engender. This is undoubtedly the chief complaint of most adults the first time they are thrust into a multimedia experience. They want to concentrate on individual images rather than to see relationships suggested by the juxtapositioning of disparate sights and sounds. Some may, and do, question whether such strange new productions belong in church.

Actually, multmedia is new only to the church. As usual, churchmen are a bit late in exploring the possibilities of this form of communication. A few parishes and leaders have experimented with it for some time,[1] but for most churches it is still virgin territory. Multimedia was born and nurtured not in the community of the saints but in the community of the artists.[2]

As early as the 1920s and 30s European and American stage artists were developing techniques of film and slide projections as background for drama. The most famed pioneer of theater multimedia is Joseph Svoboda of Czechoslovakia. In 1943, while a student, he planned a production which would have incorporated films of the actors being shown while the live actors performed the scene. Because of the war, the drama was not produced, but Svoboda has gone on to create multimedia productions for world fairs (Brussels and the Montreal Expo), operas, dramas, and the celebration of a civic anniversary (Munich). His works are elaborate affairs compared to the simple ones we'll be discussing; his "Diapolyekran" at the Montreal Expo '67 involved the use of 30,000 slides projected upon the surfaces of various cubes, everything synchronized by an electronic tape.

At the State Fair in Ohio the Bell Telephone Company has presented a popular revue on communication followed by a multiple slide show. This same company has sent out to various communities requesting it, and willing to guarantee a large audience, the spectacular "Come Take a Fresh New Look," exploring what is happening to America today. At least ten slide projectors, a film projector and stereophonic sound equipment present a "panoramic look at what's going on today with youth, race, religion, education . . . and a thoughtful look at living with change." The production more than lives up to its promise, though the "thoughtful" part comes *after* the production.

In New York City thousands of tourists have "been through the Mill" at the Burlington Mills' unique and free

---

1 See works listed in the Bibliography.
2 See Roger Hazelton's *A Theological Approach to Art* for an interesting discussion that may dispute this—the role of the artist as "saint" as well as priest and prophet to his society.

exhibit. After traveling on a moving sidewalk and observing fabrics, hosiery and rugs being woven in a working mill below, the viewer is treated to a delightful slide show of Burlington products being worn by people. Onto the top row of screens are projected heads and headgear, the next row have the breasts and trunks of the persons, and the bottom row the legs and feet. Like the old children's block game, the shifting slides make up odd people with wild and wacky combinations of apparel—for example, a policeman's head, a well-filled strapless halter, and a pair of men's shorts.

The musical *The Me Nobody Knows* also is greatly enhanced by the slides projected onto screens above the stage action. As the cast of children and youth act and sing out their hopes, dreams, and frustrations of living in the ghetto, slides of children's drawings, faces and ghetto scenes comment upon and reinforce the mood of the scene.

Rock groups and their producers have used multimedia techniques to provide "total environment" for their music. The Filmore West and East and the Electric Circus are gone now, but they and a host of imitators have overwhelmed their patrons, mostly young, with exciting visual experiences. The term "psychedelic" has been added to our language, referring not just to the drug scene but to any "mind expanding" experience launching us beyond everyday reality. Such light shows and multimedia presentations have provided drugless trips for many. The loud pulsating sound, the shifting patterns of light and color overload the senses, lifting the participant (a far better word in such an experience than viewer) seemingly into another world—what Harvey Cox has called an electronic version of the medieval mystical experience.[3]

For most churchmen the first exposure to multimedia has been at national or regional conferences. Often these have been moving experiences opening up new vistas

---

[3] See his *Feast of Fools* for an interesting discussion of this.

to those ready "to see." For others these have been confusing, frustrating occasions. We Protestants have a long tradition of ear-centered worship and education, one from which most vestiges of the visual have been eliminated. A short visit to a typical worship service or church school class will show the most popular forms of communication, the sermon and lecture. These are both what Marshall McLuhan would call forms of a "hot medium." A hot medium provides for little active involvement of the audience, the latter's role being more that of passive consumer. Most worship and educational experiences consist of talk, talk, and more talk, mainly from the pastor or teacher. Note how little time is provided for dialogue or silence in a worship service. We seem not to know what to do with silence so we cover it up with talk or organ music. Even when the pastor is avant garde and persuades his people to try a folk or rock liturgy, the result is much the same, a leader-planned and -led affair. The package has changed; hip language replaces Elizabethan in the prayers and Scriptures, the music is contemporary, but everything is well defined, spelled out in the omnipresent mimeographed bulletin. Sit back and close your eyes, for your ears will convey everything of importance to you.

Little wonder that many folks should have trouble with multimedia. It's a different ball game. There is no "right way" to view or react, only *your* way for you. As has been stated before, the sights and sounds do not necessarily follow in a linear, one-thing-at-a-time sequence. In fact, three or more stimuli are barraging your senses at the same time. Those used to "stopping the action" to think about the experience (something that many good preachers provide for in their sermons) find that there is no time for this in a multimedia production. Too much is happening that they would miss. There is only time to react instinctively, to take in what is happening and to make connections between the ever-changing images as best one can, for one combination, almost as soon as it is registered, is replaced by another, and another, and another. The person may give up in frustration, shutting out everything. He may concentrate on just one set of images, often the film part if this is used. Or he may learn to see in a new way, a non-sequential way, one in which he begins to link up diverse, usually unconnected images to create a new, changing pattern.

The kind of reaction depends upon both the producer and the audience being open and willing to try a new form of communication. The communicator must know his audience, what their experience has been, just how long and involved an experience they can absorb. He especially must have "eyes that see and ears that hear." This implies a theology of perception. We Christian educators are too prone to jump on the latest bandwagon and ride it to the end of the line before jumping onto the next one to come along (group dynamics, films, sensitivity groups, simulation games, etc.). It would be tragic if multimedia were approached in the same way, as a gimmick or bag of new tricks to prop up sagging interest among the youth. This would be to miss what it can be, a way of helping people see the paradoxes of life and to express their reaction to them.

Church educators must beware of this "leaven of the Pharisees." To enter the field of multimedia without some knowledge of what you hope to accomplish and what the dynamics of the experience are is foolish. It is still true that the blind cannot lead the blind. To enable others to see reality in new and fresh ways, the enabler himself must develop his probing, perceptual faculties. This is a joyful, even playful, task; and the best friends along the way will be the artists of our time joined with the writers of ancient Scripture.

Both seem to have the special grace of seeing reality in new ways. The author of the filmstrip *Modern Art and the Gospel* portrays the role of the modern artist as similar to the Old Testament "seer," the prophet who probes beneath the surface appearances of life to discover the reality hidden from casual view. Roger Hazelton agrees when he discusses art as "disclosure," very much akin to the Biblical concept of "apokalypsis," unveiling or revelation.[4]

For instance, the prophet Amos saw and proclaimed sickness and death, the impending judgement of God, while his contemporaries saw only healthy prosperity. Conversely, the unknown poet who wrote Isaiah 40-55 declared hope and joy and deliverance at a time when his captive compatriots could see only the death and gloom of their Babylonian captivity. Compare his great poems to the sad lament of Psalm 137 written about the same time.

In our day the ancient warning "What does it profit a man if he gains the whole world but loses his own soul" has been powerfully presented by such writers as Sloan Wilson in *The Man in the Grey Flannel Suit*, Arthur Miller in *Death of a Salesman*, and John Braine in *Room at the Top*. Painter Irving Levine depicts a gathering of prosperous looking individuals in the *Gangster Funeral*. A photograph would show little else; the artist through distortions and the use of only brown colors discloses something of the corruption beneath the surface appearances of this group, obstensibly gathered together to mourn over and pay homage to a friend—in reality one or all of them may very well have been responsible for the dead man's sudden departure.

Filmmakers from Griffith to Fellini have been quoted as making such statements as "My task is to make men *see.*" To remove the scales that encrust our eyes, to enable us to see both the despair and the joy of our situation is a great task, even a calling. The process may be a slow one so that "we see men, but as trees walking." Once begun we cannot and will not turn back. To develop a new perspective and then through our work to begin to enable others to see in new ways is to enter into what the New Testament calls joy—or the conversion experience of "being born again," "of entering the Kingdom like a child."

---

4 *Theology of Art,* Chapter 1.

Father John Culkin has written:

The arts play a new role in education because they are explorations in perception. Formerly conceived as an extracurricular luxury item, they now become a dynamic way of tuning up the sensorium and of providing fresh ways of looking at familiar things. When exploration and discovery become the themes, the old lines between art and science begin to fade.[5]

And, we might add, between art and religion. Art can be approached or seen in much the same way as the parables in Scripture. Seemingly simple anecdotes drawn from everyday life, such stories were told to a people who "have eyes but do not see and ears but do not hear." Compare this to Simon and Garfunkel's song, "The Sound of Silence," especially the stanza which describes the fruitless efforts of all those who attempt to break through the deadening silent void which separates us from one another.

The parables were entertaining and could be enjoyed on this level, as can many of the good films, novels, plays and songs today. But also they were often puzzling. "Why does he teach this way? What does he mean?" A father once asked in exasperation during a discussion of Simon and Garfunkel's songs, "Why don't they come out and state clearly what they mean? Why do poets make it so hard to understand their message?" Questions were raised, the clearest instance of this being found in the events following the Parable of the Sower (Matthew 13). The disciples don't understand the story, so they ask Jesus its meaning. They become involved in the search for the answer to their question. Luke's account of the visit of the lawyer asking about the greatest of the commandments is another good example. Jesus answers with the Shema and the commandment "love your neighbor." The lawyer agrees but continues "Who is my neighbor?" Jesus could have responded with a moralistic principle. Instead he tells the story of The Good Samaritan, concluding with the question inviting involvement, "Which of these was a neighbor

5 Quoted in "Communications Primer" by Samuel A. Eisenstein in *Sister Corita*, p. 24—see Bibliography, p. 122, for full reference). Originally published in *The Living Light*, vol. 4, no. 4, Winter 1967-68, and reprinted by permission.

to the man? ... Go and do likewise."

Spiritual truth, the Scriptures seem to claim, must
be revealed but only to those wanting it enough to
search, to quest-on for it. Some came and heard the parables ("for without parables he did not teach," Mark
claims), were amused or puzzled, shrugged their shoulders,
and went on their way. Others, searching, paused, were in-
trigued, and began to ask "What does this mean?" The
possibility for dialogue, for openness to truth, was offered
to all. Some accepted; some did not, "lest their eyes be
opened and they repent from their sins."

I have seen similar dynamics in a group of West
Virginia youth touring the Museum of Modern Art in New
York City. The art was unlike anything they had seen.
They had been forewarned of this and encouraged to ask
any questions they wanted. They had been exposed to a
few prints of works of art and had discussed them, but
that was far different from being surrounded on all sides
by unfamiliar forms of art. For some of the group it was
a fascinating, mind-expanding experience, the chief frustration being that the time was far too short. But for
several, the frustration lay in not finding any pretty or
recognizable pictures. "Why, that's just a collection of
junk. Even I could do that!" This may have been true;
only no one else but the artist had seen the possibilities
in the castoff junk or had assembled it all just that way.
They could not be coaxed into pausing long enough before
a work to ask "Why?" Hundreds of exciting works beck-
oned to them to enter into dialogue, to quest-on for meaning, and they could only ask "When do we get out of here?"
They *knew* what art is—a picture that makes "sense"—
and they were not about to waste time on such "junk."

How do you break through to such persons? Maybe
you cannot. The Gospel writers were especially concerned about this matter due to the failure of Jesus himself to reach many of his own people. But you keep trying.
The joy comes from those who *do* begin to see. A useful

Picasso, Pablo, *Guernica* (1937, May-early June). Oil on canvas, 11 feet 5 ½ inches by 25 feet 5 ¾ inches. On extended loan to The Museum of Modern Art, New York from the artist's estate. Reprint permission from The Museum of Modern Art, New York.

technique that I use at the beginning of the workshops I lead is the following:

A large print, about four feet long, of Picasso's *Guernica* is prominently displayed. The group is invited to come as close as they wish to examine it and to make a one-word reaction.

"Take a good look at this work. What is your feeling at the moment?"

"Ugh!" "Death." "Unpleasant." "Mixed up." These and the following dialogue are a composite of many groups' reactions.

"How many of you have seen this painting before or know something of its history? If you have, don't let the others in on this yet, but try to think back to your first encounter with the work. Do you have anything else to add? Does it help to see some of the other works of the artist? What types of colors does Picasso normally use? (The blacks, whites and greys are the actual colors of *Guernica*). Whatever is going on, what do you think the artist *feels* about it? What could have caused him to create this?"

By this time all groups have shared their knowledge of Picasso, but the name "Guernica" seldom rings a bell.

"What about the date then—1937? What was happening?"

"Uh—a worldwide depression. Not much else."

"What about Europe? In fact, what country was the artist from?"

"Well . . . Spain . . . *Spain!* There was a war on there, a civil war."

More facts are recalled about the war. The Republicans and the Falangists. The outside parties—the Communists and the Nazis and the Fascists. Picasso's commission to execute a large mural for the Spanish pavillion at the Paris fair.

Without going further into the events behind the painting, the group discusses the work itself. What do they see?

"People . . . in distress . . . some are dead . . . there are animals ... the horse seems distressed also ... but the bull? ... the buildings ... the flames ... the lamp ... the eye at the top, or is it a light bulb?"

Bit by bit, with a little encouragement, the group shares what they see. Puzzled expressions gradually give way to those of discovery as one person adds an insight to the whole. Most see some kind of devastation, probably the war. Usually someone comments on the stippling on the horse's body; the similarity to news print is noted. The eye or light bulb (technology?) is debated. Once a teenager noted how the painting reminded her of a Nativity scene. Since then I often ask a group if they can see any such similarity.

"There are animals and people. No star, though there is the light bulb or eye. No Mary or Jesus, unless— yes, there is a mother and child. She isn't smiling, and the baby doesn't seem to be alive. . . ."

Mention is made of the medieval triptychs, the altar paintings made in three segments or frames with the Madonna and Child in the center and the animals and admiring shepherds and wisemen in the side panels. "Look at the reproduction. Can you see how Picasso has divided his work into three major parts? Three large triangles starting at either lower corner and meeting at the lamp. Look again at the figures. Which way are they looking? Death and destruction are all around them but they seem to be looking up. Any idea as to why? What may have happened? Do you see any clue as to the source of such pain and agony?"

After coming so far, most groups are surprised to see how much they can discover about the painting without knowing much about its background. Alone each member felt puzzled and inadequate, but through the group sharing, a new confidence and understanding is built up. Most even say that they "like" the painting. Or when I show some sample of Sunday School art (*Christ in the Fields*, etc.), they find the contemporary work much more interesting. By now some of the hard facts about the city of Guernica are shared. The use of the market city on that market day of 1937 as a testing grounds for the Nazi dive bombing tactics. Picasso's rage at this wanton destruction, incarnated in this masterwork which not only protests the act itself and the new barbarism made possible by modern technology, but also warns of further atrocities to come. The stippling on the horse calls to mind the newspapers which first carried the story of the saturation bombing of Guernica, a story long forgotten in the wake of far greater atrocities committed by all parties to war—of Pearl Harbor, Shanghai, London, Dresden, Hiroshima, My Lai—but the protesting work of art lives on.

The artist, like the Old Testament prophet, does more than protest and issue warnings. At his best he also seeks some sign of hope. Look closely again at the painting. Do you see any such sign in *Guernica*? Given such explicit instructions, most groups discover it (do *you* see it?)—the flower growing out of the hand of the shattered warrior-statue. Small, delicate, almost insignificant, easily passed over, much as was that first Nativity. Where did the wise men who had some clues first look for the newborn king? Was the Crucifixion or Resurrection any more noticeable then? Were these events at the center of the picture of the Roman world or off in a corner?

The works of many other artists can be used in a similar way to involve a group in seeing and sharing. Every church should own the previously mentioned filmstrip *Modern Art and the Gospel*, as it contains excellent reproductions of rarely reproduced modern paintings. Sooner or later, however, such discussion should lead the members to create their own art. Hundreds of churches have had fun creating the "instant art" known as collages. The materials are simple—scissors, paste, paint and brushes, stacks of magazines and newspapers. Such activity can be just scissors-and-paste busywork, or it can become a means of developing a "seeing eye."

A collage is like a frozen multimedia show. It is a unified work created from diverse sources—magazine

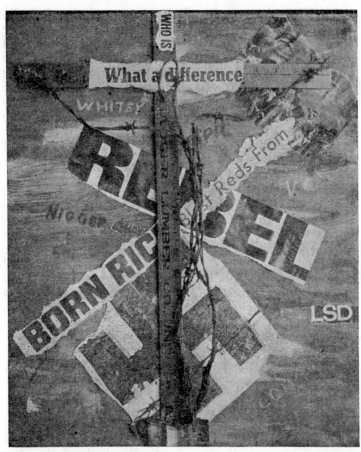

Crucifixion collage entitled What a Difference *by the author.*

pictures, words from ads and headlines, dabs of paint—all brought together so that a new mix, a set of new relationships that were not seen before, results.

This crucifixion called *What a Difference* is a far cry from Picasso, but it illustrates what can come out of a collage-making session. The youth had gathered together in the middle of the floor of a large room an assortment of paper, paints, cardboard, and junk. Rummaging through the materials, I came across the broken yardstick and a collection of hangers. Perhaps because I love puns the connection between Christ and "ruler" popped into mind. The rest followed quickly. The cross is an instrument of death, yet the ruler says something about the figure hanging upon it. The somber grey background reflects the Good Friday mood of death also. Some of our words of death can just be seen in it: "nigger, spic, whitey, commie...." In this age of public tolerance we do not emblazon such words openly, but the sickness which they represent is very much a part of our grey psyche. Around the cross we are reminded again of His words: "As you did it to one of the least of these, my brothers, you have done it to me." The twisted cross warns us that even that which is most sacred can be distorted and misused in a demonic way; the Nazis had their twisted cross, but our Klansmen still boast of their burning cross. The words and headlines say something about our world and about the One whom men call Lord of the world. Perhaps you lovers of symbolism can see the large Chi Rho. Only a few have perceived the garbage cans out of which the cross seems to rise and connected them with Gehenna.

Created out of junk, *What a Difference* has served its purpose in helping others to see the possibilities of using materials lying close at hand. Dennis Benson has urged groups to create a "theology of junk," a way of looking at and using the ordinary in new ways. This was Jesus' way of relating to people. Persons society considered as junk, unwanted castaways—prostitutes, tax collectors, fishermen, "sinners"—he saw from a different perspective.

15

His creative eye saw the kinds of persons they *could* become, beautiful sons and daughters of the living God. The wonder is not that such common men and women were able to do so much, but that we who claim to be their spiritual descendents can do so little.

Probably the artist-seer who has delighted and helped more people than any other "to see the extra-ordinary in the ordinary" is Corita Kent. An artist of our times, this former nun has produced silk screen prints combining the words of poets, philosophers, theologians and Scripture with bright swatches of colors. If poets and writers can be said to "play with words" in a literary sense, this phrase even more aptly describes what Corita Kent does visually. Her serigraphs are filled with words, large and small, many times the logos from familiar ads. She breaks them up, prints them backwards, sideways, superimposed—rearranged in unusual ways to force the viewer to look again, to observe the familiar in an unfamiliar way, and perhaps, to discover new meaning in what had been meaningless due to overexposure. At an "Arts and Communication" workshop she shared her approach by quoting Father Germann:

> We must sacramentalize in the midst of men of today. We must relocate the role of words, the inspired word, as a complement to nonverbal signs—celebrations. A simple presence is preferable to wornout words. Men of today put doctrinal statements outside their lives. Religious education must be able to open people to respond to secular signs.[6]

Jesus declared, "I am the Bread of Life." A nationally known bakery advertises "Wonder Bread—Builds Strong Bodies Twelve Ways." Corita Kent in a number of works reminds us artistically what we should have known theologically, that there is a connection between the two, between "spiritual bread" and "ordinary bread." Christ, the Eucharist—*Wonder Bread*—a fresh, new loaf. A print entitled *That They May Have Life* has, between rows of discs, the words "Enriched Bread." Isn't this just what Christians claim about Jesus Christ?

The Beatles also provide her with intriguing ideas. Whether originally created for Christmas or not, Corita Kent's *Look, Love Is Here To Stay, And That's Enough* beautifully sums up the Incarnation. Or how many pious homes display a flowery plaque declaring "Jesus Never Fails." She has taken this somewhat hackneyed phrase and combined it with Lennon and McCartney's line "I Get By with a Little Help from My Friends." The latter is printed at the top, "Jesus Never Fails" appears over a large upside-down "Open," and on the right side running down and then up the page is "It's not easy." Some real food for thought.

Ads for cereal, automobiles, a grocery company, fruit, beer, oil and gas, air conditioners—all these skillfully and colorfully blended with the words of saints and sinners. Strange and delightful are the results. But no more "far out," actually, than the "wet and wild" disclosures of God recorded in the Scriptures: the promise to an old man and a childless woman that they would produce a mighty nation; the call to Moses through a burning bush; the warning through Balaam's ass; the "still small voice" to a discouraged prophet; the weird visions of Ezekiel; the startling claim of Deutero-Isaiah that Cyrus, God's "anointed," would defeat mighty Babylon and rescue captive Israel; a baby born of a peasant woman in a stable; a public execution on a hill by Jerusalem's garbage dump. The artist, then *Sister* Corita, once stated, "Maybe Christ is showing us how to see when he says, 'Learn what the fig tree can teach you.' Today Christ might say, 'Learn what the billboard can teach you.' "[7] Or perhaps the ads in *Time* and *Good Housekeeping*.

Earlier two filmmakers were mentioned. No art form is as much of our times as this one. Thus the church enabler will find the serious filmmaker to be one of his staunchest allies in enabling people to see. Since the days of Griffith when good film directors stopped imitating stage

6 Eisenstein, "Communications Primer," p. 22.
7 Ibid., p. 26.

drama, the film has become an exciting and spectacular art form. A director, by skillful use of the camera, can make us see only what he wants us to see by blocking out all irrelevant detail. On a stage we might not see a door knob slowly turning, but the movie camera can focus closely upon it, creating a mood of suspense or anxiety. With long shots we can see the vistas of Grand Canyon, and with an extreme close-up shot, the terror reflected in a single eye.

The great themes of the Bible and theology are dealt with in a probing, realistic way in the better quality films. Alienation, reconciliation, love, hate, greed, jealousy, death and crucifixion, resurrection, rebirth. Just to think of these is to call to mind such films as *Citizen Kane, East of Eden, On the Waterfront, Edge of the City, A Patch of Blue, Billy Budd, Cool Hand Luke, The Graduate, Last Summer, Cat on a Hot Tin Roof, The Ox Bow Incident, Grapes of Wrath, Zorba the Greek*. These are but a few available in 16mm format from film rental companies.

The church enabler who is alert to what is showing at the local theater or on "(Monday) Night at the Movies" or what can be rented will find himself and his group developing new insights into the Scriptures and to life. Nor need you approach such an experience with fear and trembling any more. The literature on films is so vast that anyone can dip into it and begin to develop a seeing eye for film. Several film companies and organizations publish excellent discussion guides for the better films. We would do well to recall the claim made by several artist-critics that, were Christ to come in the flesh today, he would be a filmmaker, casting his parables in this engrossing medium.

We are called to have ears that hear, also. And there is much to hear these days. There's music in the air. Louder and with a heavy beat, but with far more substance to the lyrics than the "good old songs" remembered so fondly by Lawrence Welk fans. The lyrics need to be heard above the beat and shared. Many adults are surprised when they see and hear the words of some popular songs of the past ten years. Just as the serious filmmaker probes such themes as love and hate, peace and war, sin and justice, so are many of the songwriters displaying a new consciousness and responsibility. (Interestingly enough, some youth are also surprised to discover that the words of their favorite songs might relate to the Gospel; either they too missed the words in the midst of the beat and volume, or they just never thought that the Gospel might relate to anything so important.)

Bob Dylan, Pete Seeger, Paul Simon, Malvina Reynolds, the Beatles, Joan Baez, James Taylor—these are but a few of the sensitive writers and singers that hold the attention and loyalty of the "under-thirty generation." As with all art forms of every age a vast amount of garbage is being produced, but standing out from the trivia are songs such as these:

THE BEATLES' "ELEANOR RIGBY," which urges us to take a second look at the lonely, lost people of the city, where too often the church serves only as a burial place for the dead. Or their "NOWHERE MAN," stronger than any sermon urging the uninvolved to reconsider their fence-sitting life-style.

SIMON AND GARFUNKEL'S "SOUND OF SILENCE," probing the lack of communication in our mass communications society.

RAY STEVENS'S "EVERYTHING IS BEAUTIFUL," which is a beautiful celebration of our human differences, and thus of our uniqueness.

HARRY CHAPIN'S "CAT'S IN THE CRADLE," a sensitive lament of a father who realizes too late what his familial neglect has done to his son while he as head of the family was worshipping the success gods.

GLEN CAMPBELL'S "RHINESTONE COWBOY," a Top Forty version of "What does it profit a man if he gains the whole world but loses his own soul?"

Aided by some of the literature that has been appearing

(see the Bibliography), some church groups are mixing their theology and pop music (Top Ten Theology?) and finding both more exciting than ever before. If you have not tried this, invite your group members to bring a favorite record to a meeting. Listen to the song, look at the words if possible (several magazines are devoted to printing the lyrics of current songs), and discuss them. Some questions that may help probe the meaning or significance:

WHAT IS THE SUBJECT OF THE SONG? This may be obvious, but not always. Dylan's "A Hard Rain's Agoing to Fall," Joni Mitchell's "Both Sides Now," and Phil Och's "Crucifixion" are rich in symbolism, some of it requiring a great deal of probing.

WHAT IS THE MOOD OF THE SONG? How does the singer (or writer) feel about his subject? How does he handle it? In a straight, serious way, or satirically, tongue-in-cheek? Does the song deal with life as it really is, or does it seem to deal with a sentimentalized never-never land? This last question is important if the subject is "love"— many songs present moralistic exhortations such as "you gotta love everybody." This may be true but not very helpful if the writer goes no further by suggesting how or where we get such love. Which leads to another question:

WHAT IS HIS VIEW OF MAN? OF GOD? Any parallels —or contrasts—with the Gospel? Can you find any Scripture passages dealing with the same concern?

Church educators who have taken the music of youth seriously have discovered not only new insights into the Gospel but have also developed a rapport with young Christians obtainable in no other way. When youth see that church leaders are willing to take them and their music seriously (though not *too seriously*), they will frequently drop by and ask "Have you heard this latest disc? It's got a couple of songs you really should hear." A beautiful thing occurs—education becomes not a transaction between leader and led, but a joint venture of discovery and mutual sharing. An all too rare event in school or church.

Today even some of the comics are for those "with eyes that see." Robert Short in his two books explores the micro-world of cartoonist Charles Schultz's "Peanuts" and relates it to the larger world of theology. Breathes there a pastor so dull who has not used at least one "Peanuts" episode to illustrate a sermon? It seems strange now that a few years ago some listeners were shocked at the idea of a "Peanuts" cartoon being used in a church. The mix of secular (cartoon) and sacred (theology) was too strange for some, so accustomed to the false dichotomy between the two are we; but for others "Peanuts" in the church opened new vistas of faith and humor.

Indeed, "Peanuts" is but a part of an awakened interest in the relation of theology and humor, faith and play. We owe a great debt not only to Robert Short and Charles Schultz, but also to Peter Berger, Harvey Cox, Joseph McLelland, Elton Trueblood and Nelvin Vos for bringing the consideration of comedy and play back into the overly sober enterprise of theology. Such theologians have done their job well, as the spate of books and articles on the subject shows. It is up to us now, pastors and church educators, to translate their findings into the language and life of the parish.

We have lots of help for such an enterprise. Not only "Peanuts," so rich a treasure lode that we must refrain from the temptation to mine only its riches, but scores of fine record albums by artists like Bill Cosby, David Steinberg, Dick Gregory, Shelley Berman, to name only a few. Churchmen should be finding ways of using their devastating, uproarious comments on our human condition, the "divine comedy" played out by us and our fellow human beings. Such audio-parables can illuminate the comic situation of our society in memorable ways. No sermon on the evils of segregation could puncture the myth of racism better than the routines of Dick Gregory.

From the perspective of the Crucifixion and Resurrection of Jesus of Nazareth, the man "in Christ" can see life and death in a new way. Life is not a "fleeting moment" to be clung to, nor death a dread terminal point to be submitted to in stoic resignation. The writers of the Gospels show that it was the Resurrection which enabled them to really *see* the significance of those last events of Christ's life in a new way. Standing before Pilate, the representative of the greatest power then known to man, the weak, silent Jesus is more than meets the eye. He is th Christ who "lays down his life," Isaiah 52-53 incarnate. The raw power of priests, governor, the mob and soldiers, and the cruel death of the cross loses its power, and therefore its terror, when confronted by the One whom they cannot destroy but only manage to hold for a scant three days.

Since Christ claims to transfer this same victory to his friends, we too can thumb our noses at death. "Look, the Emperor (King Death) doesn't have any clothes on!" In the arts it is not the tragic vision, viewing man as doomed to destruction because of a fatal flaw, which is closest to the Gospel. Rather it is the comic view, depicting the incongruity of what man claims or pretends to be and what he actually is. Life on this side of the Resurrection is best portrayed not by brooding Hamlet, but by Chaplin's Little Tramp, battered and bumbling but still retaining a semblance of bruised dignity.

Such a view enables us to celebrate life, or better the Author and Redeemer of life. An important part of such celebration, and of creativity, is playfulness. Harvey Cox, in commenting on the work (or play, the two seem to blend together in her life) of Corita Kent, says:

> What does she do? Well, instead of being defeated every day by being inundated by the countless messages from the mass media, she plays with them. She twists them around. She puts them in new configurations. She puts them into juxtapositional relationships, so that once again the human is asserted, not by getting rid of the mass culture but through a playful approach to the culture.[8]

Although the above describes the serigraphy of a former

---

8 "Corita: Celebration and Creativity" by Harvey Cox in *Sister Corita*, p. 18. Copyright 1968 by United Church Press. Used by permission.

nun, Dr. Cox could be describing the process of creating multimedia. From the mass of messages and materials that assault our senses, we select a few (hundred) that might help reveal what is hidden—ads, posters, photos of current events, songs, voices—play with them, try out different combinations, rearrange them in new configurations, reject some, choose others, and finally, many hours later, hopefully arrive at an absorbing comment "asserting the human."

If you are willing to undergo the discipline of the arts, you can develop the necessary insight for producing multimedia. Especially when you work with a group, such fears as "I'm not creative" will begin to melt away. There is a great line from the film *Why Man Creates,* which every Christian should see, to the effect that creativity is the ability "to look at one thing and see something else." This "something else" is what the members of a group can help one another see. Each person can make his own contribution, whether in producing or in discovering the meaning of a multimedia production, the most important contribution being simply the support and encouragement of brothers and sisters in Christ.

It is time that those who do not practice speaking in tongues discover again the power of the Creator Spirit. We need to reassert the claim that every Christian has the gift of the Holy Spirit, even if we do not use the "Pentecostal" label. If we really believe that we are created in God's image, that we become "new persons in Christ," and are called "to live and walk in the Spirit," we will find a new source of creativity within and among us not thought possible before. Too many Christians "poor mouth" their talents, in reality dishonoring the work of God and shortchanging the work of the Spirit. Many self-styled ordinary, "untalented" children of God have come alive in the middle of a group that has become convinced that God's Spirit does indeed impart gifts to those who seek them. If the New Testament is correct, God's children, baptized into Christ and recipients of the Spirit, are a "gifted people."

GADGETS, GIMMICKS AND GRACE

Why not find this out in your own congregation? Multimedia is not the only way for this to happen, but this ought to be the goal of any use of the technique. Used with caution and tender loving care and discipline, your media work-play might become an effective channel for the Spirit.

On the Brink
of Multimedia

Slide Show

Some day the cartridge slide projector will be found in as many churches as is the filmstrip projector. Perhaps in a different form, one combining the best features of both. Filmstrips are convenient to store and easy to handle, which is why in the past they have won out over the sets of slides once offered to the churches. However, they have one drawback which is a serious limitation for the creative user. Each frame is locked into a sequence, someone *else's* sequence. There can be no rearranging, no creative possibility of using them otherwise than as intended (except, of course, of using a different sound track or incorporating them into a multimedia production—more on this later).

Many possibilities for creating tailor-made presentations are open with a collection of slides. The same slides that are used in a stewardship presentation can later be used, in a new combination, in an interpretation of the Bible or as a part of a worship service. Compared to filmstrips, slides offer great freedom for the user, the only limiting factor being his own imagination. And this latter will grow and grow, as I have discovered, the more he enters into the fascinating world of media.

A good way to begin,[1] especially with youth, is to attempt a song interpretation. Youth might prefer a popular song and adults, a hymn. My appetite was first whetted when a group of senior highs from a small church in Iowa presented a slide show at a pastors' conference. Wanting to interpret their music to adults, they had selected three or four "top ten" songs, such as the Beatles' "Revolution," and had worked for several months preparing slides which were cued to the words. Accompanying the presentation and inviting discussion afterward, the young people had put together such an outstanding production that they were invited to share their show with numerous churches, service clubs and community groups around town. Their attempt to help adults understand the teen world through its music resulted in a moving, memorable blend of media and method.

Whether you choose a hymn or pop song for interpretation, the lyrics should suggest visual possibilities. Not every good song does this, as my own youth group discovered. The first time our senior highs attempted this, they chose the Fifth Dimension's "Declaration." No one will dispute the beauty of the words of "The Declaration of Independence." They are noble, lofty, true. But they are *not* readily translated into visual form. At least not in one night—we were using the "lift-off" method of slide making (explained in detail later), which allows a beginning group to create a slide show in an evening. After a lengthy, futile search for suitable pictures, they gave up and chose an alternate—"Bridge Over Troubled Water."

Simon and Garfunkel's beautiful song is almost too visual. That is, the words themselves suggest such specific images that the interpreter could settle for a series of slides of lovers and bridges. In other words, a too literal interpretation which adds or suggests little that is fresh

---

[1] Some "packaged" youth programs that involve such visual techniques will be discussed in the chapter on resources.

or new. Most of those with whom you work will probably produce this kind of interpretation at first. This will introduce them to the techniques of the slide show: setting down the lyrics on paper, cueing the slides to words or phrases. But this is only the beginning, as the sequence from "Peanuts" on page 28 suggests.

If he can find a supportive group, even poor Charlie Brown will be surprised to find himself seeing more than "a ducky and a horsie" in the clouds. With encouragement, prodding, and sharing of enthusiasm and insights, many a person has been excited to discover the creative potential within himself. Your role of group leader can be to help each member make this discovery. And you will be surprised at how creative you yourself are becoming in the process.

For "Bridge Over Troubled Water," pictures of lovers and bridges may be in order, but do not stop with such obvious images. Are there other dimensions to the song, other possible interpretations? Any parallels in Hebrew-Christian literature? Check out the books of Hosea and John. Now whose image might the song suggest? "Like a bridge over troubled water, I will ease your mind." How about slides focusing upon parts of a bridge, such as two trusses forming a cross or a chi? Other possible slides: black-white handshake; people embracing; scenes of the Crucifixion and descent from the Cross ("Like a bridge over troubled water, I will lay me down"); posters of love and hope (in the manner of Corita Kent's delightful print *Yellow Submarine*, combining the Beatles' song with the traditional symbol of the Church—a ship). Once a group started off on such an interpretation, all kinds of possibilities for visualizing the song would be discovered.

The above suggests a straightforward treatment of a song. With slides you may also want to make an ironical statement at times. Such a visual statement can make clearer than any words the contrast between what is and what ought to be. An ideal song for this is the folk hymn that has swept through the churches, "They'll Know We

PEANUTS® By Charles M. Schulz

Are Christians by Our Love." A beautiful, haunting song. But does it reflect reality as we experience it in our congregations? It does not require a Madeline Murray O'Hare to remind us how far short the life-style of so many of us falls from the ideal proclaimed in the song. A priest once said that he could no longer enjoy this hymn; he had seen far too many boys lustily singing it in chapel, only to commence gleefully beating each other up on the playground five minutes later. Do adults fare better—or do they just become more sophisticated? A little imagination, especially when shared in a group, will turn up many possible visual comments on the words—scenes of rioting, segregation ("and we'll guard each man's dignity ..."), an ornate church building followed by scenes of poverty.

Or maybe you are with a group of adults who would prefer a more traditional hymn. "Onward Christian Soldiers" is great for a Mad Comic style interpretation. Many of us today find it hard to sing this song with a straight face, so alien does it seem to reality, and so often has it been parodied in words. "Onward Christian *Soldiers*"? Does the average church member really see himself in this role—a person sent forth on a mission? "We are not divided, all one body we"? When some towns have churches on four corners like gas stations competing for customers? A quick succession of shots of five or ten of the churches in your area would say more at this point in the hymn than any sermon on ecumenism and the divided churches.

Perhaps your group wants to explore the theme of freedom. The lovely song "Born Free" is open to a light treatment to underscore a serious purpose. Every town is filled with "no, no," signs: "No Parking," "No Loitering," "Keep Off the Grass," "No Trespassing," and so on. Send the members of your group out with cameras to photograph such signs. Ask them to look for signs of positive statement also. They may be surprised. A succession of such slides shown with the flowing melody and words of

29

the song should make any discussion of the theme of freedom more lively.

Thus far we have seen some possibilities of simple song and hymn interpretation. Slides and music also can be an intriguing way of probing the Scriptures. The emotional flavor can be heightened in a powerful way, far more so than by words alone. The Bible lends itself to this kind of treatment. The Hebrews thought in very concrete, visual images. Modern scholars have often stated that the Biblical writers are poets rather than scientists or objective historians. Almost every book of the Bible is filled with visual imagery, posing problems of interpretation for the modern reader. Yahweh, Lord of the heavens, which sing his praises and declare his glory, is the One "who stretched out the heavens," "who rides upon the storm." He is the "Shield of Israel." He takes "Israel by the hand and upholds him with his mighty arm." He is the brooding, wronged Bridegroom of an unfaithful Ephraim. The Old Testament is crammed with such images.

"Shepherd," "green pastures," "still waters," "paths of," "valley of the shadow of death," "rod and staff," "head with oil," "cup," "days of my life," "house of the Lord." These are by no means all of the suggestive, visual words of even one of the shorter Psalms—Number 23.

The Gospels also are filled with visual imagery. Study Jesus' favorite (and according to Mark, only) method of teaching, the parable. Anecdotes, metaphors, similes appeal to the imagination of the hearer, inviting him to share in the quest for spiritual truth, rather than to passively receive it. "Who is my neighbor?" he is asked. We might reply with the statement of an abstract, philosophical principle, which may be one reason why most of our sermons are dull for children. Jesus responds with a story, a parable for those "with eyes to see and ears to listen." A story that really does not end until he asks "Which of these three was a neighbor ... Go and do likewise."

John adds his own touch of poetry-theology to that of

Christ. Note such phrases unique to his Gospel: "the light still shines in the darkness, and the darkness has not overcome it"; "I am the door"; "I am the true vine." A hurried skimming through the New Testament will reveal many such passages, even in the more abstract letters.

A junior high group, wanting to open up the Parable of the Prodigal Son, decided to work out a slide interpretation. First, they read the passage, discussed it, and wrote the key words upon a blackboard. For each word they searched through stacks of magazines for small pictures that might interpret the concept. After selecting and cutting them out, they made them into slides using the lift-off method. They listened to various songs—such as "Five Hundred Miles"—which expressed the feeling of lostness (they had decided to concentrate on this aspect of the story). The words of the song and of the parable were then written down with the slide cues indicated. During all this activity, the leader kept exploring the meaning of the passage with the group.

This same youth group produced another "show" incorporating slides, Scripture and music for an Earth Day program. They spent a Sunday afternoon traveling around the city with their cameras. They snapped pictures of factories, dumps, litter, trees, flowers, scenes of beauty and ugliness. Another Sunday afternoon the group chose Scripture passages—two of the nature Psalms—and songs, Pete Seeger singing "My Hudson River" and "This Land Is Your Land." Deciding upon an order, some of the young people recorded these on a tape. Others wrote the words down for their script. Finally, four of the kids met to select the slides to be used. The adult leader was out of town, leaving the youth to meet with his wife. None of the little group felt secure in the venture, but the result—an eight minute production involving about a hundred slides shown with two projectors—was a moving, visual statement of concern about our imperiled planet and community. Many of those in attendance at the Earth Day Banquet described it as the most meaningful portion of the program. The group has since been invited to share the fruits of their imagination and work with various churches and groups.

But why should kids have all the fun? Adults also can produce such experiences, once they learn the basics of visual language and get over their "but I'm not creative" hang-up. Some of the tasks they are called upon to undertake in the church could be much more exciting with a little "holy image-ination." Teachers and youth advisors will see many possibilities, but these are not the only ones who can turn on to new methods.

Many women are called upon to lead Bible studies and mission programs for their women's groups. Usually, as evidenced in many churches by declining attendance (and the advancing age of those who do come), these are rather dreary sessions. Someone reads from the study book. The questions are read half-heartedly. Smiles. Silence. One or two responses declaring the obvious. Feet shuffle. Quick glances at watches, the floor, the clock on the wall. End of lesson—and of ordeal for another month. "Now we will have our coffee and cake." Suddenly the room is abuzz again, as it was before "the lesson."

Almost as bad, though more hopeful, are some of the attempts to bring new methods. The leader has read about "audiovisual aids" in her literature. She sends for a filmstrip. She is busy that week and so has little time to study the filmstrip in advance. Just a quick glance at the script. Thus, after almost jamming the projector at the beginning (unless she has snagged "The Reverend" to run the projector), she has trouble matching picture and sound. Several ladies complain they can't hear. Again some of the printed questions are read. Silence, for the most part. "That was nice. Thank you for getting this. The pictures were lovely."

The above two scenes, hopefully, are caricatures, but they may be close enough to reality to make some readers uncomfortable. How different the scene might be if the study leader first determined to try a fresh approach. She might invite a few friends in and try out her ideas over coffee. Others she might consult are teenagers (for music) and the pastor, the latter for support or theological insights. If it is a Bible study, questions as to the central theme, context, the emotional tone, and implications of the text for today could be explored. With one or more persons, perhaps those who have been heard expressing their discontent with the usual approach to Bible study, ideas would more easily start to flow on how to share the exploration with the larger group.

For discussion purposes let us say that the study is from the Sermon on the Mount. Each section of this offers many visual and aural possibilities for exploration. Much of the music of our day is concerned with ethics, human relations, and discovering meaning in life, which is just what Jesus' Sermon is all about. Zeroing in on one passage, look at Matthew 6:24-34. After study and discussion, you conclude that Jesus is speaking about the quality of a person's life, the danger of a life centered upon *things* as compared to one built upon trust in a loving God. A quick glance through the many women's magazines will show just what he is talking about—and reveal many excellent small pictures, ads and words that can be made into slides by the lift-off process. You might choose to make a tape of someone reading portions of the passage, combined with verses of a hymn or song. Slides of food and fashion ads, interspersed perhaps with those of weight reducing gimmicks, words, people's faces, household gadgets, and other sights would make this a memorable way of opening up the Scripture for discussion.

Mission and stewardship programs are other projects in which church members are often asked to participate. Fortunately, the films and filmstrips now produced by national offices are better than the terrible, saccharine things thrown together a few years ago by so many church boards. However, you need not rely exclusively on ready-made audiovisuals for effective presentations. A set of slides, with appropriate music, of the local church and

33

community, of familiar faces carrying out the teaching, preaching, visiting, worshipping work of the church would be effective.[2] These could be used in conjunction with a filmstrip on the worldwide mission of the church; or, if the strip is yours, frames from it could be cut out and mounted in slide frames and incorporated into the set of slides. Voices of your people—pastor, officers, choir, youth —could be worked around or over the music.

Last of all, does your annual meeting need a little excitement? Instead of only telling about the past year (people can read mimeographed reports later if they are really interested in statistics), why not present a slide program depicting most of the highlights of the year—the special worship services, weddings, youth events, picnics, family nights, etc.? Touches of humor can be added by inserting special slides (e.g., "our youth group"—a riot scene; "our youth advisors"—riot-equipped police; "a meeting of our official board"—scene of the General Assembly of the United Nations; "our pastor"—a shot of Billy Graham or Pope Paul; all of which can be obtained from back issues of news magazines with the lift-off method). Such a presentation requires planning a year ahead and having someone with a camera present at all major events (and some routine or minor ones as well). The result would be well worth the trouble. Who knows? The little band of "the faithful few" that always enable the church to barely make a quorum for the annual meeting might swell to a group actually looking forward to the event.

The above are a few of the possibilities for home-brewed visuals. Once you try such a project, and the congregation responds positively, new ideas will come to mind. New possibilities for exploration will open up. Requests to lead a study or "give a devotional" then are no longer dread chores to escape or to obediently endure. They become

---

2 At least one denomination (United Presbyterian) offers a set of slides on the worldwide mission program of the church with places for a local congregation to insert its own slides. Check with the national stewardship or audiovisual office of your denomination to see if they offer anything similar.

challenging opportunities. Such excitement is catching. It can even be one way of experiencing the Holy Spirit.

Your slide "shows," short and amateurish at first, will become more polished with experience. You will start trying out different techniques, such as using two slide projectors. You are then on the brink of multimedia. You are ready to plunge into that jarring, confusing, yet fun-filled, world of intermix of films, slides and sound. Before we take the plunge together, however, we need to take a closer look at the humble yet basic building block for your productions, the lowly slide.

The Lowly
Slide

Multimedia Building Block

Filmmaking seems to be the "in thing" with many church educators now (while their more avant-garde colleagues rush to buy Sony videotape systems). Too often the lowly slide is overlooked, which is a serious mistake. As rewarding and as exciting as filmmaking is (and we will have something to say as to its possibilities later), it is still somewhat expensive. Nor is it as accessible to a group as slide making. For either slide shows or multimedia productions, slides are media man's best friend, a basic building block.

In this chapter we will be discussing two broad categories of slides, those made without and those made with a camera. Most good media productions will involve a mixture of the two kinds, but if your group is starting out on only half a shoestring, by all means learn how to make slides without a camera.

A. SLIDES WITHOUT A CAMERA

Mention of the lift-off method has been made several times, so we will begin with this kind. Any group having access to a slide projector (hopefully a cartridge type, though our youth were able to use a filmstrip projector with its slide adapter) can put together a set of 100 slides for about $3.00. Even bargain buys of camera film can never equal that!

The process is so simple that even children can learn it. (If I start working on slides when our children are up, I can expect our five-year-old to ask "Can I make me a slide?" The process is such that with help at strategic points he can make one.) Materials needed:

1. CARDBOARD SLIDE FRAMES available at a camera store. Ask for the 127 or 135 size. (The "size" refers to that of the opening. The outer dimension is 2″ x 2″ for both, thus fitting all standard slide projectors.) These are available in boxes of 100 for slightly over 2¢ apiece. If your camera store develops slides, you can probably purchase these in boxes of 1000 for 1½¢ each.

2. CLEAR "CONTACT PAPER," which you can buy under other brand names also at department and variety stores. The price will range from 35¢ to 49¢ a yard.

3. SLICK PAPER MAGAZINES OR CATALOGUES.

4. A PAN OF WATER.

5. AN IRON AND A SMOOTH BOARD.

Using the slide frame as a guide for size, select a small picture, ad or words that will fit within the opening of the frame. The 127 size is the largest opening, and hence the most useful for our purposes. (Slide frames with various shaped and sized openings—down to 16mm—can be bought.) *Time* and *Newsweek* are excellent sources for pictures since they use so many small ones with their articles. The major limitation of this method is seen here: the size. Whatever you want to turn into a slide must fit into the frame opening. The picture should have good color contrast and sharp outlines if it is to project well. Color pictures will turn out fine, though light pastel shades may appear somewhat washed out when enlarged.

After you have selected and cut out several pictures, cut the contact paper into strips just a fraction of an inch larger than the frame opening. A series of dots or other markings on the glue side of the frame will indicate how far the transparency should overlap. The glued surfaces of the frame must come into contact all around, so do not make the transparency too wide. Failure to do this properly will leave one side of the slide unglued, causing it to jam later in the projector.

On each strip of contact paper mark off the same width. Cut along these marks. You should have a stack of small squares slightly larger than the opening of the frame. This procedure will save you from the time-consuming chore of trimming each transparency to fit properly later.

To peel the paper backing from the contact paper, tear one of the edges slightly. The paper will tear but not (usually) the tougher plastic transparency itself. Touch only the edges, unless you want a large, personalized fingerprint in the middle of your slide. There is no way to remove this, so take care.

Carefully grasping the edges of the square of contact paper, hold it over the picture so as to place it on the desired portion of the illustration. This positioning must be done before the stickly side of the transparency and the paper come together. It is possible but very difficult to peel a badly positioned picture from the contact paper; very likely the paper will tear unless the removal is done slowly. When you have the position you want, lower the transparency to the picture.

The working surface for this step should be perfectly smooth and hard. Start rubbing the transparency from the center out to the edges. Use your thumbnail (some prefer the bottom of a spoon) for this. Apply considerable pressure so that you will remove all the air pockets and tiny bubbles. By holding the picture so that light is reflected from the surface, you can tell when the process is finished. Those portions of the slide that look grayish or slightly mottled need further rubbing. The areas without air bubbles will appear very clear by contrast. This step is *very* important and worth taking extra time; at the workshops I find that more potentially good slides are ruined by eager beginners hurrying through this step than by anything else.

When you are certain that you have rubbed out all the air bubbles, immerse the slide in a pan of water. The temperature of the water does not seem to make any significant difference. The picture should be completely covered by water. Since it requires from five to ten minutes for the water to loosen the slick, clay surface of the paper and to "lift off" the ink, go ahead and repeat the process with other pictures. (I usually wait until I have from twenty to fifty pictures before making slides—it saves a lot of time.) As you place your ninth or tenth picture in the pan of water, your first ones should be ready to take out.

Often the original paper will float or peel right off the transparency. This will vary from magazine to magazine. Sometimes you must remove the paper by gently rolling or rubbing a finger over it so that it comes off in pieces. The ink will remain on the transparency as long as you do not use your fingernail and scratch the surface.

Careful examination will reveal a grayish film on the sticky side of the transparency. The clay residue can be washed away under a faucet. Or you can dip your fingers into water and wash the deposit away, using a towel or lint-free rag both to clean off your fingers and to blot the transparency dry.

The penultimate step is to take another square of clear contact paper (there is an even clearer variety made without glue on the one side that works just as well—and so will clear sandwich wrap), take the backing off (if you use the sticky kind), and place the two squares together, sticky side to sticky side. Again using your thumbnail, rub out the air bubbles. You should now have a transparency smooth on both sides. This second layer of clear contact paper will protect your slide from fingerprints and dust.

The final step in slide production involves your iron, heated to a medium-low temperature. Position the transparency in the frame, keeping it within the guidelines (you will often have to trim the transparency). Fold the two sides of the frame together, and press firmly along the *edges* of the frame with the iron. For obvious reasons, do not iron the transparency itself! You are now ready for that first awesome view of a slide made by your own hands. A moment to remember.

The process, complicated sounding perhaps, is simple once you have tried it a few times. The "lift-off" method is just that. The ink in slick paper productions is not actually printed on the paper but upon a thin coat of clay covering the paper. The water dissolves the clay, allowing the ink to be lifted off by the glue of the contact paper.

The resulting slide will not be quite as clear as one made with a camera, except for words and line drawings. Clarity will depend upon the original printing process. The finer the dots making up the picture, the clearer the projected, and enlarged, image will be. Usually, the pictures in news magazines will be coarser than those taken from a publication such as *National Geographic*; often such pictures, mixed with clear ones made with a camera, will add interesting variety to the production. Words, line drawings and cartoons will turn out the clearest of all.

Poster catalogues can provide you with colorful slides interpreting a theme or thought. Argus Communications prints the most attractive and useful catalogue. Words of love, faith, hope, and challenge are beautifully underscored by the art—and the reproductions are, for the most part, just the right size for slide making. Play fair with them. Order some of their posters as well as their catalogue. Posted around the room before your presentation, these will intrigue your viewers when they see them incorporated into your m-m experience.

B. OTHER NON-CAMERA METHODS

The write-on way is probably the oldest and most widespread method of slide making without a camera. Most

GADGETS, GIMMICKS AND GRACE

camera and large school supply stores sell blank slides that can be written upon by anything that writes—pens, pencils, Magic Markers, crayons. They vary in price from a nickel to over 15¢ each.

If you use acetate inks, you can make your own blank slides out of clear contact paper. Words, color patterns, lines, etc., can create just the right effect necessary for your production. You can even type upon contact paper, a covenient way to make titles. The ink will smear, so you will have to use three squares, the one typed upon sandwiched between two others.

Even mimeograph stencils will work, the letters appearing white upon a dark background. Should you know someone with access to a transparency maker, you may want to experiment with it. Any picture, and in the large models this would include those from books, can be copied as a transparency. Intended for overhead projectors, the large sheets would yield quite a few 2″ x 2″ slide transparencies. (More on the use of overhead projectors later.)

C. SLIDES MADE WITH A CAMERA

Few and far between are the homes without some kind of a camera, especially the ubiquitous "Instamatic" type. Whatever the brand or type, as long as slide film is made for it, you have at hand a tool that should be used in the church more. We will be discussing cameras, though not in great detail—there are plenty of books and magazines with technical information—in the chapter on resources and equipment. What follows is a treatment of the kinds of pictures needed for media shows.

If you are knowledgeable in photography, you are ahead of most of us. In the workshops I conduct I always stress that when I first began to produce slide shows, my only camera was an Instamatic, and the sum of my knowledge of film and photography was contained on the small sheets packed with every roll of film. I still do not know much more than this, but I am learning, and a large number of people have testified to the effectiveness of my ventures into multimedia. In other words, to underline what was said in the Preface to this volume, you do not need to be an expert to attempt a media show. You do not wait to become one and then dare to create a slide or multimedia experience. You gain knowledge through some study—such as this book—consultation with a camera fan, perhaps, but mainly by plunging in and learning as you go. A pastor acquaintance is an excellent photographer, one of those persons who fusses over every detail of a picture and is satisfied with nothing but the best. Certainly, these are admirable qualities, but also deadly. He has never tried a slide or multimedia production. He was upset by one at a conference. Apparently the creator had little plan or order, and worse, for my friend, some of the slides were below his standard. Although the quality of the slides should be as high as possible, too much professionalism can paralyze a person. A slide will be viewed from a half to eight or ten seconds in most productions. It should be interesting, well-composed and lighted, and clear, unless you are consciously trying for a softer hazy effect. If you select only flawless ones, you will never have enough time to assemble a show. My friend will probably never produce a multimedia production. Too bad. He is missing a great opportunity.

You will need pictures of people, of faces and hands; of places and events in your community and church; of celebrations; of trees and hills and flowers; of children; of signs and billboards with unusual art or slogans (one of my favorites is a shot of a large billboard of the Purity Bread Company proclaiming "Purity Does a Body Good!", a saying that could have come from St. Paul's Letter to the Corinthians). Record anything that strikes your interest. Don't worry at first how you will use the slide. A good practice is to carry a camera with you in your car just in case you come across something interesting as you travel around town.

Although unstaged pictures are usually the best, you

may wish to set up special scenes. Use your imagination to create photo collages—scenes combining magazines pictures or bulletin covers as a backdrop and objects in the foreground such as a cross, cup and loaf of bread, creche figures, etc. A portrait or close-up lens will probably be needed for such a scene, but the small investment will be well worth it.

With a portrait lens, even an Instamatic becomes a more flexible instrument. Slides of pictures and magazine covers can be made. With a slightly better camera and close-up lens any painting or picture in a book or magazine can be reproduced as a slide. The whole world of far-off places and events can now be incorporated into your production.

Filmstrips are good sources for slides. Many churches and denominational offices have stewardship and promotional strips lying around gathering dust because of outdated content. Yet locked into their sequences may be just the right scenes you need—pictures of people helping others, of mission stations, foreign cities and buildings. Cut out the frames you want and slide them into a cardboard or plastic frame (half-frame size) purchased at your local camera shop. Filmstrips on the church, racism, pollution, world missions and a host of other subjects are available. (See the chapter on resources for some specific suggestions.)

Perhaps you have just purchased a good filmstrip and are not ready to cut it up. If you own a single lens reflex camera with an interchangeable lens, the purchase of a slide duplicator, attachable to the front of the camera in place of the lens, will enable you to copy another slide or frame in a filmstrip. (Again, more on this under "Resources and Equipment.")

One word of warning: slide making is contagious and may be dangerous to the health of your pocketbook. There is no end to making, compiling and using slides. You may have to restrain yourself from using them for every occasion. You soon begin to think visually. You may then be ready for the multimedia plunge.

44

Getting It

All Together

Multimedia Producing

Slide shows are useful and fun, but once a person has seen a multimedia show he begins to yearn for broader horizons. To take off from an old song, how are you going to keep them down to one projector after they've seen nine in operation?

Professionally produced shows at fairs and conventions have both helped and hindered the growth of "grass roots" multimedia. Many of us now creating our own first saw the possibilities of multimedia at such events. However, others came away declaring, "Wow, that's great, but we could never do that!"

There are multimedia productions, and there are multimedia productions. The reader *might* have access to nine projectors. If so, more power to you. (And I mean that in an electrical sense also—watch those overloaded circuits!) The media productions we will be describing in this chapter and the next are far simpler than the professional ones you may have encountered. Few churches are without access to *some* audiovisual equipment. They are more limited by the imagination and derring-do of their leaders than by lack of hardware.

If we define multimedia as a "show" involving three or more pieces of equipment, then the simplest form will use a tape recorder and two slide projectors. Two slide projectors do more than merely double the number of images. With one projector, contrast had to be achieved in one of two ways—a slide could clash with the words of the narration or song, or with the slide preceding it. Scenes of love and hate, war and peace, beauty and ugliness must alternate with one another sequentially. But with two projectors they can be shown at the same time, creating a more potent, upsetting mix.

Of course, a similar effect can be achieved with one projector by a "split screen" technique. Two contrasting pictures can be laid together side by side and photographed. This is effective, often done in filmstrips, but the contrasts are always locked into the same frame. With two projectors one slide, let's say of a lovely mountain lake, can be held on-screen while a series of contrasting shots—of litter, pollution, urban blight—flashes on and off. Then another slide is held on the opposite side and a series of contrasting scenes is shown.

A two-projector show offers many possibilities but is simple enough so that even the most staid, visually naive audience will have little trouble in grasping it. All of the occasions discussed in Chapter 2—Scripture and song interpretations, stewardship presentations, etc.—lend themselves to this treatment.

Many leaders use three slide projectors for their presentations. A professional travelogue lecturer, an ecologist, a freelance church enabler, a British architect—these are some whom I have met who work exclusively with this combination. All delight in the variety of combinations such a system can provide and also in the "cinerama" effect of blending three slides of a scene into a spectacular panoramic view.

Introduce one or more movie projectors into this, and you have a more controversial mixture. Even some media producers disapprove of this, claiming that the mere fact

46

that a film *moves* draws too much attention to itself and away from the slides. And yet at least one artist works only with films, his feature length films requiring three movie projectors! My own first attempt at multimedia uses two films and one set of slides.

Signs along the Way is an eighteen-minute exploration of the call of Christ to discipleship in the midst of the swirling, numbing events of our day. Using a set of 240 slides, an 8mm and a 16mm film, it is as fast paced as the times. Thus far about sixty groups around the country have experienced it in one of the two kit forms in which it is available. What follows is a brief description of the experience, a composite of some of the reactions of the audiences, and the "how" of production:

"No man is an island, no man stands alone . . ." To a gentle guitar accompaniment the Montfort Singers (now the Mission Singers) sing John Donne's great affirmation of the solidarity of the human race. Slides of people caring for and helping one another, words of love and celebration follow each other across the screen. To the right of the slides a Laurel and Hardy film depicts Stan with his girl friend pretending not to hear the knocking of Oliver and his female companion outside the door. The episode foreshadows the strong denial of the idea that "we need one another" soon to follow in a Simon and Garfunkel hit. Meanwhile, to the left of the slides a series of television commercials silently unfolds: ads for paper towels, breakfast cereals and drinks, coffee, etc., etc.

The soft song of affirmation ends, and the voice of D. T. Niles underscores the message as he urges us to become "captive to the vision that sees beyond the Cross, His and ours and the world's, and to discern that which the Cross itself makes possible. We must be alert to hear the cry which rises from the ground. . . ." We see in the slides those new crucifixions about which the theologian is speaking—scenes of war, segregation, rioting.

No sooner does his voice fade away than the denial of the affirmation sounds forth in the rock song by Simon

47

and Garfunkel, "I Am a Rock." The singers describe in stark detail the results of retreating from life's loves and pain to a rock-like existence that must eventually lead to a living death. Love, friendship, laughter—all such joys are shut out of the inward fortress within which the spirit holds itself a prisoner.

Slides of lonely people, posters and traffic signs ("Bridge Out," "No Parking," "Stop," "Dead End"). A TV minidrama shows Grandpa, the old raisin snitcher, sneaking into the dark kitchen pantry. He clutches a box of Raisin Bran to his breast. He rips into it, greedily sorting out the raisins. Suddenly the lights go on. He is discovered, caught in his diabolical, raisin-snitching act—by his grandson. We laughed at this on television (and remembered to buy Raisin Bran at the supermarket). We do again, but now, in company with the slides and song we see that there is poignancy, even sickness, beneath the humor. Grandpa's greed is harmless enough in an affluent society. But how funny would lovable ole Grandpa be in a concentration camp where the scarcity of food could be a life and death matter?

The result of such rock-like withdrawal from human contact and concern unfolds as we hear Martin Luther King, Jr., speaking in Birmingham. He urges his people to continue their struggle against racial injustice despite the silence of "good white people." More slides of people demonstrating for freedom, enduring the indignities heaped on them by men of hate. The TV commercials continue on and on. Men may love and hate, kill and make peace, but there will always be one constant—that of buying and selling. By now the 8mm film is depicting the events of that horribly fascinating year of Our Lord 1968, a year in which Dr. King figured so tragically.

Two harsh voices almost break in on the civil rights leader, "Hell, I don't have any sympathy for them . . . this is America . . . I just don't understand what all the trouble's about. In America anybody can make it who's free, white and twenty-one!"

"We shall overcome, we shall overcome . . ." Pete Seeger leads a Carnegie Hall audience in a song from another era. An era which believed that the Kingdom of Love and Brotherhood would come if enough people of good will worked hard at the task.

The civil rights anthem fades out, and a song depicting still another problem arises. "Air," from the rock musical *Hair*, amusingly welcomes in the noxious fumes and gases polluting our atmosphere. Racial scenes are replaced by those of ecology. To the left of the slides we watch as two glamorous people puff ecstatically on their Kools. The jarring incidents of 1968 continue to parade before us.

As the singer of "Air" chokingly concludes her song, Simon and Garfunkel again come on, softly singing their famous version of "Silent Night/Six O'Clock News." Over the second verse a voice is heard reading part of the Nativity story; then the harsh staccato of machine guns and bomb bursts, the sound of marching feet and the words of Jesus on his way to Golgotha, "Daughters of Jerusalem, do not weep for me. No, weep for yourselves and for your children. . . ." Slides of the Nativity, of Picasso's *Guernica*, of the Vietnam War, rioting in the ghetto, the massacre at Kent State, the Crucifixion. By now the sounds of warfare and soldiers' voices ("Kill, kill!") almost completely drown out the words of "Silent Night." In the midst of this we hear Jesus' words to his disciples, "Love one another as I have loved you!" Corita Kent's print *Be of Love . . .*, the Crucifixion, a sleeping baby. The 8mm film depicts scenes of the Nativity and the visit of the wise men, reinforcing the slides and tapes.

Another song from *Hair* asks the question of our life-direction or destiny: "Where Do I Go?" The Dameans offer an answer in their song about the invitation of Jesus, "Come In, Children, Lay Your Burden Down." Slides of street scenes, posters, children, ads. Now the commercials have given way to more serious public service spots—messages for CARE, Project Hope, Church World Service.

A news announcer flashes the news of an earthquake

in Turkey. A rapid-fire series of vignettes follows depicting how aid is rushed by Church World Service to victims of disasters—not only in Turkey, but in Haiti and India also. Shots of people helping people pour forth—Red Cross workers, CWS teams, ships, planes, CARE and CWS posters. Finally, the climax of the program, a Christianized version of Bob Dylan's "The Times They Are A-Changing." The slides of love and hate, faces of the great and ordinary, road signs, billboards, ads and posters keep pace with the musical challenge to join the risen Christ who demands that we choose him above all else.

Both films by now have focused in on the theme of the song and slides, helping to pull things together. The 16mm film concludes with a girl dancing before a large Church World Service poster as she urges us to "Love," "Care," "Act." The 8mm film is now in color with quick shots of scenes and signs of crucifixion and resurrection.

The lights come on. The projected part of the experience is over, but the "seeing" has just begun. Reactions vary widely. "My heavens, what was it?" "Beautiful!" "I don't get it!" "Wow!" "I wanted to laugh and cry—sometimes both at the same time." "I didn't know which to watch." "It sure makes you think." "Who had time to think? Everything moved too fast."

The purpose of a rap session—and some reaction period should always be provided, even if only a few moments of silence during a worship service and a discussion later—is not to get people to like what they experienced or to learn the "right" answers. Rather, it is a time for sharing—of their doubts and questions and frustrations as well as insights. Even those who express initial confusion are often surprised at how much they, as a group, are able to see and understand. Such an experience usually underscores the vital necessity of the Christian fellowship in coping with and figuring out the complexities of today's world. More than once I have heard someone complain, "There was so much going on that I became confused. Things moved too fast." To which someone else would reply, "That's just like life, isn't it? We never can seem to keep up or find time to figure it out." The discussion, then, should be allowed to happen, each person encouraged to express his honest feelings and invited to share what he saw.

Producing a multimedia is a time-consuming but stimulating experience. Here are some hints that can make the task easier:

SOUND TRACK: If you start out with a short, one-song multimedia production, you can get by with a record player alone. This will be awkward at best and impossible for a longer production, hence a tape recorder is a must—the best you can buy or borrow. A major complaint from audiences at any kind of AV presentation is the frequent lack of sound clarity. For a working copy of the audio, a recording made on a small cassette or via the microphone of a reel-to-reel recorder will suffice. However, for the actual production, you will want to record the music directly with a patch cord connection. This direct recording method will be free from room noise and distortion. Check the manual of your record player and tape recorder for instructions as to how to do this on your specific equipment. If your record player does not have an external jack for this purpose, look for the speaker (or speakers if you're recording from a stereo player; a good mono system is easier for this). You should be able to see two wires attached to two tabs or terminals at the back. By connecting two "alligator" clips to these you can run a line to the external input jack of the tape recorder, enabling you to make a direct recording. If, as was the case with myself, you know next to nothing about electronics, admit it, and find someone who does. He could be a teenager, or an adult, who never thought that his knowledge could be used in the church. Usually such persons are glad to help, especially when they understand the purpose of your project. For a more detailed explanation of this procedure, including a diagram, see Chapter 6.

The music and voice tracks for *Signs along the Way*, to

get down to the case at hand, were chosen from a large stack of records. (Your problem will not be the scarcity of suitable songs but the overabundance.) I had a clear idea in mind of what I wanted to say through this production (created for our annual breakfast for graduating high school seniors), but not of how I wanted to say it. The form began to take shape after listening to numerous songs and looking at the lyrics of even more. Some of the major problems of life today were well represented by the songs. For variety voice tracks were interspersed. The order selected was an alternating affirmation and denial:

"No man is an island..."
"I am a rock, I am an island..."
Dr. King—The bigots

Several recordings of Dr. King are now available, at least one (of the March on Washington) showing up frequently in the "three-for-a-dollar" bin at discount stores. The Lutherans have put out an excellent kit called *People, Emotions and Riots*; the voice track and many of the slides for the racism section of *SATW* were taken from the record and filmstrip of this. The voice of D. T. Niles came from the record accompanying one of the monthly issues of *New* (see the "resources" chapter, p. 114), and the conversation of the two white racists was part of an Episcopalian radio spot. This latter was on a tape reel, which required my borrowing another reel-to-reel machine in order to both play and record it.

The hardest segment of *SATW* to record was the "Silent Night-Vietnam War" episode. Originally a portion of an excellently conceived record depicting the horrors and irony of war (also from an issue of *New*), it was dubbed directly onto the tape. However, the plastic disc did not provide the best quality sound, and this was readily apparent when the tape was used in a large room. People could hear the carol and the sounds of war, but not the words of Jesus which were read. I had to redo this using Simon and Garfunkel's version of the carol recorded on one track of the tape. We backed up the tape and at the proper place on the second track recorded the sounds of war (from a sound effects record) and my voice (via a microphone) reading the words of Jesus. Played back on a stereo tape machine, the two tracks blend together in just the right way. A stereo recorder makes such sound mixing feasible even for amateurs.

THE SCRIPT: After the basic idea is conceived and sketched out, the search for ways to concretize it begins. This may include writing original material, selecting suitable songs and music, voice tracks and sound effects. Once these are put in order and recorded, you are ready to prepare the script. (This is the order followed for *SATW*; it is also possible to work out the script first and then make the recording.)

For short productions there may not even be a need for a script, but for longer affairs some kind of printed instructions should be available for the technicians. This may be simply a listing of each sound segment with the length of time each slide is to be held on screen and the cues for any other projection or light equipment used.

SATW is more complicated in that the slide changes are cued in with the words of the songs and speeches. Sometimes the slide matches the thought of the words, other times it contrasts with or denies them. Thus all the words of songs and speeches were typed out on the left half of the page with the cue words underlined. The number of the slide, printed on the right half of the page, is matched with the number printed above each cue word. The slide projectionist can keep a running check to make certain that slides and words are matched; thus others than the creator of the production can show it.

Some media folk like to run all the projectors themselves, believing that each showing itself is a new act of creating. There is no one way to do a show—whether you are a free spirit working without a script or a carefully organized person who marks everything down on paper—just so long as your method communicates what you intend to your audience.

THE SLIDES: Enough has been said previously about this media "building block" that we need not delve too deeply into the subject again. Those for *SATW* are a mixture; some were made with a camera, others cut from filmstrips, and many made with the lift-off process. Even while the idea was germinating in my mind I began gathering slides that I thought might be useful and stored them in a special box. Thus by the time the audio portion was finished, I had several hundred unsorted slides on hand. Using a large table top for my working area, I dumped them out and began to arrange them in stacks for each segment of the script. These were then arranged in proper order to go with the word or phrase I wanted to emphasize. I still had to make a number of slides but not nearly so many as I would had I not been collecting them all along. There were many, of course, which I could not use; one has to avoid the temptation to use *everything*. A useful tool for this sorting-out operation is a slide sorter, usually a translucent plastic affair with a light bulb behind it. A child's drawing scope or your church's mimeoscope works just as well. Both devices are used for tracing drawings by shining light from a bulb through paper or a stencil laid out on a surface of frosted plastic or glass— and thus they work equally well for slides. I have often seen them at garage sales and secondhand stores for less than a dollar. Load your sorted slides (after marking the cue words on your script) and run through them with the tape. This will show you where adjustments need to be made; at some points you may have too many slides, and in other places you may need to add more because of the bridge music or a miscalculation as to the tempo of the song. Once you have completed this and have made your final selections, number the slides, a simple process that will save you much grief later in the event of a spill.

THE MOVIES: As was stated in the description of

SATW, a series of television commercials and public service spots were spliced together on an 800 foot reel for the 16mm projector to show to the left of the slides. (The source of these and other possible 16mm films are discussed later.) The mood rather than the exact idea or words of the songs and speeches was matched.

A copy of Castle Films' *News Parade of 1968* forms the heart of the 8mm film shown to the right of the slides. In fact, at first this was all that was used; but there was a problem. Since it is but twelve minutes long, this meant that it was not started until six minutes after everything else had started in order that all would end at the same time. From time to time, however, additional footage was added. First a short comedy at the beginning, then some lengths from an old, dreadful film depicting the Nativity, and finally some color shots I made from paintings of the crucifixion and posters of celebration. Each segment had to be inserted at the proper place to match the songs and words; this was done simply by starting the tape and film at the beginning, stopping them both at the point where the insertion was to be made in the film, splicing it in, and continuing on to the next point. Finally, a rerun was held to make sure everything was timed right. (More later on film splicing and the wide variety of 8 and Super 8 mm films available.)

The one slide and two film projector multimedia show, as can be seen from the above description, is fairly complex to view but not unduly difficult to produce. Nor does it exhaust the range of possible combinations. Just as some m-m producers like to work with three slide projectors, others use three film projectors.

For example: Corita Kent has produced an engaging film about one of her art classes visiting a tire dealer's store to discover the overlooked beauty in the commonplace. Three 16mm projectors are needed to show the "film." The center film carries the basic line of action, with each of the films on either side zooming in on particular details, or at times emphasizing the point of the center film by duplicating the scene. The effect is engrossing; the viewer feels like a small child visiting his first toy store. The three cameras, often showing the same thing from different angles, focus our attention upon the tires, the patterns they sometimes make, the colors and shapes of the signs and letters. We see quite ordinary items in new, refreshing ways.

Another such three-part film is offered for rent by the Division of Mass Media of the United Presbyterian Church. *Change* shows what is happening in medicine, technology, ecology, and our concepts of God.

At least one filmmaker is producing story or fictional films with this technique. Dr. Edward De Roo describes his *At Ease, Charlie*, a "military odyssey" of a young draftee:

> My experiments were fictional in content with set characters involved in continuous development as found in full-length feature films. But my audiences see three aspects of the characters along with simultaneous viewing of flashbacks and flash-forwards in story telling. A conventional feature film is strung out in a once-upon-a-time literary linear progression on one screen for at least ninety-odd minutes. The audience rarely has to work hard except at eating popcorn. This is spoon-fed cinema. On the other hand, my audiences either tune in and work very hard under a three-screen barrage of information or give up and turn off.

> One common complaint is that no matter how hard the audience works, there is the frustrated feeling of missing things, especially the exact story, while watching three screens. The answer: one is always missing things, even with one-screen viewing. All art asks the viewer to return and see it again.[1]

Such extensive filming may be out of reach for most churches because of the cost—from $4 to $5 for a 3½ or 4 minute segment of regular or Super 8mm film. And this is assuming no loss due to ruined shots. If you do have several cameras, projectors and perhaps a financial angel, this method offers many intriguing possibilities worth ex-

---

[1] *Bolex Reporter*, vol. 21, no. 2, "At Ease, Charlie—A Three Screen Experiment," pp. 6-7 (see Bibliography for full information).

ploring. A somewhat less expensive alternative would be to shoot one film and a series of slides of the same scenes. The film could be shown in the center and the appropriate slides on either side.

The last suggestion leads us into the description of another multimedia kit called *Promises, Promises, Promises, Promises*. It uses a mixture of sound, from a specially prepared tape and the sound track of a 16mm film. Two slide projectors project the two sets of about 185 slides on either side of the 16mm film. The twenty-minute experience takes the viewer through some of the multitude of promises made to us daily by admen, politicians, preachers, medical shamans and others.

As the room is darkened Kate Smith's familiar voice belts out that potent blend of piety and patriotism, "God Bless America." Following the first verse the volume of the taped music begins to recede, and the four title slides, each reading "Promises," come on. In between we see and hear a candidate tell us what he will do if we elect him governor of West Virginia. He no sooner finishes than another candidate promises us that he will end crime in the streets if we send him to Washington as senator from Ohio. These are followed by TV spots promising us "sex appeal" if we use this brand of toothpaste or after-shave lotion, or happiness if we buy this toy or "stop the war," purchase government bonds, support education, rinse our hair, eat this particular cereal, wash our clothes in the latest NEW soap discovery, use the newest medical discovery, and so on and on and on ad nauseum.

Underneath the voices of the commercials the taped music can just be heard as a counterpoint—songs such as "Battle Hymn of the Republic," "Where Have All the Flowers Gone?" "We Shall Overcome," "Turn Back O Man, Forswear Thy Foolish Ways," "America, the Beautiful" (while a CARE spot shows a stark famine in India), "Sound of Silence," "O Come, O Come Emmanuel." The latter hymn begins to rise in volume, and that of the film track decreases until the taped music dominates. A voice

GADGETS, GIMMICKS AND GRACE

booms out, "Ho, everyone who thirsts, Come to the waters;
And he who has no money, Come, buy and eat!.... Why do
you spend your money for that which is not bread, And
your labor for that which does not satisfy?" This is followed by the final promise made through the song "Put
Your Hand in the Hand of the Man from Galilee" amidst
slides of celebration and of Corita Kent's mural *Beatitudes*
and of public service spots on the theme of Love.

In the above experience the film becomes the primary
factor, with the slides and taped music, except for the fi-
nale, serving as reinforcement or counterpoint. Some of
the slides are repeated for emphasis at various points
(visual punctuation). The emphasis or contrast to the
film passes back and forth from one set of slides to the
other. For example, one section looks like this:

LEFT SIDE SLIDES	FILM AND TAPE		RIGHT SIDE SLIDES
156 "Adult" movie post-ers	*Ultra Brite* toothpaste 30 sec. spot	"O Come, O Come Emmanuel"	156 *Macleans* toothpaste
157 *Playboy* ads			157 Cross & Revlon
158 Stripteaser			158 Sexy cologne ad
159 Whirling carnival ride	*Coca Cola* spot—pretty seascape	(*sound begins to dominate*)	159 "Intimate" ad
160 *Old Spice* ad			160 Close-up of coins
161 *Coke* ad		"Ho, every-one who thirsts..."	161 Poster "I Thirst"
162 Poster—"Flying"			162 Banner "God's Love"
163 Mosaic of Christ			163 Ad "People Care"
164 Cross at Coventry Cathedral		Isaiah 55	164 Crucifixion

A stop watch or clock with a large second hand is a must
for this kind of a production. So that the taped music
would come in at the right moments under the sound track
of the film, only certain verses of most of the songs and
hymns could be used. In the case of several songs, various versions were timed, the one with the most suitable
length being chosen for the recording.

Many films available at a local library or from a film
company could be used with sets of slides in the above
manner. The life and meaning of Christ could be interpreted at a retreat setting using such films as *Parable*
or *It's About This Carpenter*, especially if your group is
already familiar with these two films. Members of the
group could create slides and a tape of words and music

to be used with the film.

Perhaps your budget will not allow you to rent such films (the amount would vary according to the film and agency—perhaps from $5 to 25). There are many excellent filmstrips on the life of Christ, the history of the Church, Bible stories, the mission of the Church and the like. Your church or a neighboring one probably owns a number of these; once they are shown, they can seldom be shown again until the composition of the group has changed. But they could be used again in this new way with sets of slides serving as commentary on the filmstrip itself, the latter giving the necessary continuity and "message." You may know a camera buff who owns a slide and filmstrip duplicator. Some of the key scenes of the filmstrip can be duplicated as slides, enabling you to underline major points by showing three images of the same scene at the same time, or by recalling the scene via the slides at a later point in the presentation.

Thus far we have discussed productions using slide, movie and filmstrip projectors. We should also mention the possibilities afforded by opaque and overhead transparency projectors. I have never been fortunate enough to serve in a church owning such equipment, but if it is available to you, try experimenting with it. The lift-off method can be used to make large transparencies as well as slides. Thus large pictures can be used with the overhead projector. Media specialist Nancy Carter[2] suggests an intriguing effect created by placing a clear glass baking dish (the square or rectangular type) filled with water on the transparency projector. By dropping tiny amounts of food coloring into the water a swirling mass of colors will be projected onto the wall, very effective for certain moods and effects.

A large opaque projector will permit the use of pictures obtainable only from books or in large format size (and which you perhaps discovered too late to allow for the time of shooting it with a camera and sending off to be pro-

2 For the full treatment see her article listed in the Bibliography.

cessed). If you do use such equipment in addition to slide and film projectors, your tape volume will have to be of good, loud quality in order to be heard above the noise of the machines.

We have by no means explored all possible media mixes yet, as the next chapter will show; but before proceeding further, let's pause to recapitulate. The following dos and don'ts can save you much grief.

1. DON'T USE M-M FOR EVERY CHURCH EVENT. It is not suitable or appropriate for every occasion; much time and sweat is required to produce a good one (from 40 to 100 hours). Better fewer but well-produced events than a spate of hastily conceived and thrown together productions.

2. DO START WITH A SHORT ONE. It will be easier on you *and* your audience. Educated audiences are built up by those who know what they can and cannot assimilate.

3. DO HAVE CLEARLY IN MIND YOUR MAIN IDEA OR THEME when beginning, but don't be afraid to shift direction if the material seems to be leading in another direction.

4. DO PREPARE YOUR GROUP FOR THE EXPERIENCE through prior publicity and discussion, but withstand the temptation to tell them what to look for. Give them the freedom to make their own discoveries (you'll be surprised at times at what they see but you had missed as creator of the event) and even to become confused or upset.

5. DO USE THE FINEST EQUIPMENT POSSIBLE in making your audio tapes.

6. DO CHECK OUT THE SOUND SYSTEM BEFOREHAND, especially when showing your masterpiece in someone else's building.

7. IF POSSIBLE, USE TWO DIFFERENT ELECTRICAL CIR-CUITS. Always check where the circuit breakers or fuse boxes are located, just in case a zealous Martha in the kitchen turns on an electric coffee pot while all your equipment is on. (This happened to me once, and not even the pastor knew where the fuse boxes were, so beware!)

8. KEEP BOTH A FLASHLIGHT AND EXTRA PROJECTOR

BULBS CLOSE AT HAND.

9. DO CHECK OVER YOUR SLIDES PERIODICALLY. Straighten out or replace any that are badly bent or dog-eared. Learn how to unjam the slide projectors and how to reestablish a loop in the film if it jumps out of position in the movie projector.

10. DO REHEARSE THE PRODUCTION WITH YOUR HELPERS to make certain everyone understands their cues for turning lights and equipment on or off.

11. DO NUMBER YOUR SLIDES even if you plan to show them but once in that order. Thus a last minute spill need not be disastrous.

12. DO NUMBER YOUR SLIDE TRAYS when using more than two, and lay them beside their projector in the proper sequence to insure quick changeovers.

13. DO NOT PANIC IF SOMETHING GOES WRONG. The calmness of your faith in the face of technical disaster may communicate as much to a sympathetic audience as the production itself.

14. DON'T JUST "SHOW" YOUR PRODUCTION. You are not in the entertainment business. Seeing a multimedia production is only half the event. The shared response of the people completes the experience, reinforcing again the Biblical emphasis upon the joyful fellowship of the people of God.

15. DO, IF YOU WANT A GROUP—SUCH AS YOUR YOUTH—TO BECOME INVOLVED IN PREPARING THEIR OWN M-M, EXPOSE THEM TO ONE YOU HAVE PREPARED OR RENTED. Often it is by seeing and hearing one that others become excited about doing their own.

From Multimedia

to Mixed-Media

The visual experiences described thus far we have arbitrarily called "multimedia." Their effects are achieved by projected images and sounds. Add live actors, readers, dancers and you have, in the words of the admen, "taken a good thing and made it even better." In short, mixed-media. The mix can include not only people but things, such as banners, posters, incense—you name it. If you think that we will be spending most of this chapter discussing worship possibilities with mixed-media, you are right.

Actually, any worship service could be described in terms of a mixed media experience—a rich matrix involving words, music, symbols and pictures (often stained glass ones), and sometimes even touch, taste and smell, as when the Lord's Supper is celebrated. Harvey Cox has even referred to the Eucharist as "the first form of pop art":

... You take a piece of bread, or a cup, and put it in a very unusual setting, namely the High Mass. You lift it up and look at it. And from then on you never see bread and wine in quite the same way again.[1]

Most people are not used to thinking of worship in such terms. All churches are not equally stimulating visually. Church naves range from the severely austere, clean-lined white room of a Colonial or Quaker meeting house to the splendrous cathedral of the Roman or Greek Catholics with stained glass windows, statues and carvings, paintings and banners, brassware and richly robed priests.

Let's think, though, of what confronts Mr. Average Christian on a Sunday morning as he enters his "sanctuary." A smiling greeter or usher thrusting a bulletin into his hand. Rows of pews facing forward. The eye is drawn to a large cross above an altar or table, or perhaps there is a painting of Christ or a small stained glass window dominating the chancel area. The table is embellished with grape vines and the words "In Remembrance of Me"; on top is an open Bible flanked by two candles. To one side is a large pulpit with various symbols carved or emblazoned in color upon a parament. A baptismal font stands nearby, also decorated with appropriate words and symbols. The chancel is decorated with fresh flowers and the ever-present American and Christian flags.

The early sound mix of rustling paper, creaking pews, shuffling feet and muffled voices is soon swallowed up by the sound of the piano or organ prelude; if our "average" church is down the economic ladder, but not *way* down, the soap-opera-like tremolo of an electronic organ assaults the air. Hopefully, the music is well chosen to prepare the listener for the coming encounter with the living God. The music stops and a call to worship declares their purpose in gathering together. The people rise singing a hymn of praise. Robed choir and minister process down the aisle, emulating the ancient throngs who, chanting

---

1 "Corita: Celebration and Creativity," p. 20, in *Sister Corita.*

their Psalms, marched up to the Jerusalem Temple so long ago.

The visual mix of the chancel is increased many fold by the robes and stoles, the expressions of joy or routine boredom on the faces of the pastor and choir. Their enthusiasm, or lack of it; the gestures and tone of the pastor; his posture—all enter into the consciousness of the worshiper. The mix, like warmed-over stew, may be so familiar that it goes down with little thought. For some such traditional worship services remain satisfying; for others the exciting possibility of experiencing "the God of Abraham, Isaac and Jacob" is lost in the midst of meaningless ritual and sterile practices.

Although this is not primarily a treatise on worship, we cannot ignore the interest and controversy surrounding the subject. By describing the opening of a "typical" service of worship, we are trying to show that the worshiper is already in a mixed-media environment which through many years of exposure he has learned to accept, enjoy and support. If he is older he may remember a time when candles, robes, printed bulletins and the like were deemed too "high church" or "popish" by his elders, but now he can hardly imagine a service without them. (I am obviously describing a "typical" middle-of-the-road Protestant service.) He adapted to such innovations. And if they are introduced carefully and with love by leaders whom he respects and trusts, many of the mixed-media suggestions of this chapter can be used on special occasions in our "typical" church.

Each person desiring to use multi- and mixed-media as part of worship will want to think through his own theology of worship clearly, and hopefully, to share it with the lay leadership of the congregation (so that liturgy once more becomes the "work of the people," but that's a whole subject in itself!). There are too many traps in mixed-media to rush into it unthinkingly. Projectors and recorders can become means of the revelation of God's judgement and grace. They can also become as we have

warned before simply novel ecclesiastical toys, gimmicks
to keep the customer satisfied—especially the young, who
"must be won back to the church." Yes, they must be won
back to the authentic people of God, but not to an organi-
zation which they cannot respect because of its triviality
and lack of spiritual depth. The producers of Hollywood
films, light-shows and rock concerts can handle electronic
gadgetry far better than we in the church.

However, we do not need to be as fearful as the author
of a recent book *New Forms of Worship* seems to be:

> We must say a few words about the use of technical means,
> such as slides, movies, tapes, and various combinations of these,
> in sermons. Frankly, this is dangerous business. The power
> of these media is so engrossing that they can easily make the
> sermon seem pale by comparison. There may be occasions on
> which a single slide or a few slides may accompany a sermon.
> But motion pictures will not accompany a sermon; it instead
> will accompany the motion picture. There may be rare occa-
> sions in which a portion of a motion picture such as "The
> Gospel According to St. Matthew" might replace the sermon.
> Motion pictures ought to be left for Sunday evening discussion
> groups or other occasions. At present we do not consider mo-
> tion pictures an asset to preaching. Even when a few slides
> are chosen to support the sermon, they ought not to draw atten-
> tion to themelves but be subordinate to what is said. If we
> show a single slide of a war casualty, the emotional shock may
> be so great that nothing we say may be heard.[2]

Mr. White renders fearful testimony to the power of
visual images, which is the point we have raised in *favor*
of using them. Even though his book shows that he has
a nodding acquaintance with the theories of Marshall
McLuhan, he still thinks that media and method are separate, distinct entities, a mistake that is not only bad
theory and practice but even worse theology for one who
is supposed to be helping others declare a Gospel of the

2 James F. White, *New Forms of Worship* (Nashville: Abingdon Press, 1973), pp. 193-194.

Word becoming flesh. Words are "pale by comparison," nor should we fear to follow the example of some of the Old Testament prophets who sought to communicate God's truth through the best media they could discover—acted out parables, the bestowing of strange names on their children, the interpretation of dreams. Although Mr. White's warning about "this dangerous business" is needed to keep us from becoming media freaks in the chancel, we need not let his uneasiness with the media prevent us from declaring the Word through such means *when the topic or occasion is right*. (And only you and perhaps some of your perceptive leaders can gauge this!)

All this is to say that mixed-media should grow out of hard thinking and planning for worship rather than being stuck in to add spice and interest. Of course, no matter how much preparation, some will be offended. But careful preparation will minimize this reaction; thoughtless interjection will guarantee it.

Let's assume that you have thought through your theology of worship, prepared your people, perhaps by using multimedia at family nights or as a part of study groups, and are now ready to take the plunge. First, of course, what are the physical realities of your church nave? Can the windows be darkened so that projected images will show up well? If not, can the service be moved to another large room without too much disruption? Or is a vesper service more in order? When does the sun set and darkness descend? How good are the acoustics? Are there enough electrical sockets? Enough wall space or floor space for screens to be set up, dancers or speech choirs to do their thing?

More important theologically, in which parts of the service do you want to employ your mix? The traditional liturgy is rich in possibilities: the sermon (we list this first only because most usually think of this), the Confession and Absolution, the Scripture lessons, an anthem, the Offertory, a reading or litany of dedication.

Since the sermon possibilities are so obvious (much of

what was said in an earlier chapter about slide presentations will apply here), we will concentrate on the other elements of the liturgy and conclude by describing several mixed-media experiences.

PRELUDE/INTROIT A slow-moving series of slides for meditation. No doubt most people would prefer nature scenes, but well-composed slides of the city and of the church should also be used to offset the tendency to deify or romanticize the country. The Argus posters are designed around well-chosen quotations; one or two slides made from these would offer much food for thought if tied in with the theme of the service.

THE CONFESSION A break from the usual printed unison prayers would be welcomed by most worshipers. Confession can be offered to God on behalf of the people in the form of a brief dramatic vignette, a dance interpretation of a prayer or song. At a youth rally a group danced as a boy sang selected portions of the hit from *Superstar*, "I Don't Know How to Love Him"; at another a group interpreted the Beatles' "Eleanor Rigby." A series of slides, shown in silence or accompanying words or music, even dancers, can powerfully portray our sin—poverty, war, racism, pollution—as long as you remember that this is to be a prayer and not just an opportunity to rub people's noses in their dirt. A series of faces can be very effective, features contorted by rage and hatred, dulled by alcohol or poverty, wracked by grief and pain. The congregation may reflect on these or respond with some form of the "Kyrie" or other response.

THE ABSOLUTION The traditional words so often used for this, once fresh and communicating the fantastic Good News that God loves us in spite of what we do, seem pompous and stilted to many Christians today. What should be a high point of the service is missed by many, preachers included—by the very ones who are burdened down with feelings of guilt and frustration. At this point, then, we would especially urge that some creative thought be expended to emphasize what should be such a great moment in the drama of worship. The very words of Scripture are needed, assuring us of God's great love, but their tone and flavor can be beautifully enhanced by a few well-chosen slides. A church nave with a cluttered front but a lovely, blank wall at the rear was the scene of a celebration concluding a youth rally. After the Confession the liturgist declared that God in Christ loves us, calling us to turn around from our sin and follow him—at which point the congregation, standing, did just that. Facing the back of the room, they were greeted with scenes of love and joy flashed forth by two slide projectors. The old Scriptural assurance was heard again, but with a difference, even as to posture and position.

THE OFFERING At a conference the worship leader divided the group of thirty-five or so of us into small groups. One of our tasks was to think about our experiences together and to give thanks to God by writing or drawing something upon the "write-on" slide that was given us. Pencils, Magic Markers and crayons were made available. The offering plate—a carousel slide tray—was passed, and each of us dropped our slide in. To the familiar strains of the Doxology each slide was shown on the wall; words of love, hope, joy, a number of well-executed designs and short quotations enhanced the service, bringing us all to a deeper awareness of what it means to "render unto the Lord." An alternative for a larger service would be to show slides, during a quiet offertory song, of some of the many things and events from our daily lives for which we are thankful. The more ordinary the better—a cereal box, a parent and child embracing, a lovely treat—just look around and all sorts of subjects will suggest themselves.

THE CHARGE Some congregations are foregoing the King James style benedictions for charges to the people of God, urging them to go forth into God's good, but hurting, world and to fulfill his mission entrusted to them— slides of work, play and worship (the later in the narrow, usual sense, that is), of home and school, of people caring for and helping one another. As with the Absolution described earlier, the congregation may be facing the door at this point symbolizing their embarking upon their mission.

Such are some of the acts in the drama of worship and a few of the many possibilities open to those who would seek again the excitement of the weekly encounter between God and his people. Let's see how a few of these fit together as a means of celebrating the presence of the living God, again for the purpose of stimulating your own ideas. Both services were held at a festive occasion calling for a special kind of celebration: the first at a youth rally and the second at an annual organists' meeting and, in a modified form, at a state council of churches annual meeting.

How do you plan a worship service to follow a dance with a rock band? With difficulty? Not necessarily. The dance was a part of a youth rally called "Choose Life." This is what happened late that Friday evening:

The band was good—the youth for the most part needed no coaxing onto the floor—so the music was allowed to go on for an extra half hour. Finally, the music stops, most of the band put away their instruments, and several of them form a folk singing group. By now the more than 350 youth and adults are seated on the floor and join in the singing. Several songs later the lights begin to go out as the group sings "Sound of Silence." The hall grows silent as well as dark. With only a candle for a light, one of the leaders reads from John's Gospel, "In the beginning was the word . . ." As the reader begins the second verse, someone turns on a radio at low volume. Several members of the congregation stir uneasily. The DJ's voice and blaring music are familiar, but not in *this* setting. No doubt some of the adults are wishing someone would grab hold of the kid rude enough to interfere.

The reader starts on verse three: ". . . all things were made through him. . . ." The volume of the radio rises. A second one is turned on, tuned to a different station. A newscast is in progress. The voice of the reader rises, trying to climb above the level of the music and announcer. "... The true light..." "The latest report from Vietnam..." "La da da da—boom boom..." The reader, no longer heard above the cacaphony, finishes the fourteenth verse, stops, extinguishes the candle. The radios are cut off at the same moment. Sudden silence. Darkness. A nervous hush, broken only by the rustle of bodies shifting position.

Then music. A choir sings "Alleluia" over and over as Ed Ames's powerful voice chants the opening of the song "Who Will Answer?"

Images appear on a large wall. The Castle Newsreel of 1968 unfolds the horror of that insane year. Two slide projectors show scenes of man-made chaos. As Ames sings about the threat of atomic holocaust, two filmstrip projectors are turned on, increasing the number of projected images to five. Part II of the filmstrip *America, America* shows "the other America," the side that never appears in the strip's song "America the Beautiful." The other filmstrip projector shows the "Guernica" section of *Modern Art and the Gospel*—scenes of the Nazi dive bombing attack on the Spanish city interspersed with detailed views of Picasso's great painting. "Who will answer?" indeed! The terrified women in the painting seem to shriek this as they gaze toward a God-less sky from which comes not angels from heaven but mechanized death creating a hell on earth.

The soloist keeps hurling forth the question contained in the song's title: "Who Will Answer?"; and the choir responds with the repeated Hebrew praise-exclamation, "Alleluia!" Silence again. Even the words of the song reveal the paradox of our times. The darkness of men strives against the light of God.

Live singing now. The folk group starts up again with Simon and Garfunkel's "Sound of Silence." The voice of the reader comes over them with "The people who walked in darkness have seen a great light..." He reads through Isaiah 9 to verse 8 and stops. By now the singers are just

71

beginning the third verse about the multitude of people speaking yet not communicating. The reader takes up Matthew 13:10-16 (the Phillips paraphrase, omitting v. 12): "You shall indeed hear but never understand, and you shall indeed see but never perceive..." The singers continue, "And the people bowed and prayed..." The reader begins Luke's account of the Parable of the houses built on rock and sand. The last chords die away as the reader concludes "...and the ruin of that house was great." The message of Scripture and song have blended together in the minds of those present, each helping to interpret the other.

A few of the room lights come on. The liturgist again reads John 1:1-14. The congregation responds with the folk hymn based on the passage, "The True Light That Enlightens Man." This song, too, is an unexpected blend of the familiar—of Scripture and the folk melody "Michael."

A group reads antiphonally Psalm 150. "Praise the Lord... Praise him with trumpet sound... Praise him with timbrel and *dance*..." Robert Edwin's recorded voice is then heard in his superb arrangement of Sidney Carter's hymn of invitation: "I danced in the morning when the world was begun... Dance then wherever you may be, I am the Lord of the Dance said he..."[3] Three girls present their rhythmic interpretation of the song. For most in the congregation it is their first taste of liturgical dancing. Some of them will get to know the three dancers the next day in the Dance Workshop. A large cross looms in the background. The dancers appeal to the congregation, back and forth, whirling, facing and pointing to the cross, then the people; at the conclusion their taut bodies arch toward the cross.

The recorded music ends, and the congregation takes up the song, "... dance then wherever you may be; I am the Lord of the Dance said he, And I'll lead you all wher-

---

3 Copyright 1963 by Galliard Ltd. All rights reserved. Used by permission of Galaxy Music Corp., N.Y., sole US agent.

ever you may be, I'll lead you all in the Dance said he."

The lights are on. Jesus' charge is declared: *"You* are the light of the world! Let your light so shine before me . . ."

All stand and pass the Peace with the singing of "Shalom, my friend, Shalom my friend . . . We'll meet again, We'll meet again . . ." A full evening of listening, discussing, dancing, singing, and now celebrating ends on a high note. The congregation disperses to their guest homes for the night.

The above contains little that is really new. Only the mix is different, a mix that was not thrown together like a stew of leftovers, but one whose ingredients are carefully measured out. The second mix was created for an entirely different type of group, an annual meeting of the local chapter of the American Guild of Organists. The leaders wanted a program on multimedia. Instead of a "show," they agreed to a worship experience involving all the senses, for the Lord's Supper would be observed. Again, the somewhat detailed description is given not to brag of past accomplishments but to stimulate your thought. It would be unwise to try to duplicate the entire service, but certain parts may be useful in your parish.

After an opening hymn, a choral group reads from Norman Habel's "Invitation to Worship":

Now is the time to live,
to come to the Father who creates us,
to sing to the Lord who frees us,
to dance with the Spirit who fills us . . .[4]

The lights go off. Silence for a moment. Then we hear a deep bass voice from the Creation segment of James Weldon Johnson's "God's Trombones" (the Roy Ringwald/Fred Waring recorded version) describe in naive yet touching terms the story of Genesis 1. As the creation of light is referred to, the two slide projectors start showing

---

[4] From *Interrobang* (Philadelphia, 1969), by permission of Fortress Press. Anyone seriously interested in contemporary worship should have all of Habel's excellent books!

slides of the sun, stars and moon, the seas, plants and animals, mountains, a rainbow and a storm—all on a large rearscreen system. A 16mm projector shows a film of a potter creating a vase on his wheel.

The poetic sermon comes to its moving climax with the account of the creation of man, and the tape recorder and movie projector are shut off. The slide projectors show a couple of slides matched with the passage from John 1 read by one of the choral group members. "In the beginning was the word . . . The light shines in the darkness, and the darkness has not overcome it." The reader finishes, and the song "Light Sings All over the World" bursts forth from the tape recorder. A series of slides of sunrises, posters of sun faces, pictures of Christ, and happy scenes cascades forth from the slide projectors. The song of affirmation (sung in the Broadway play *The Me Nobody Knows* by a group of ghetto children) fades out, and our reader, flashlight and Bible in hand, reads John 1:9-17: "The true light that enlightens every man was coming into the world . . . grace and truth came through Jesus Christ."

Organ and choir commence Bach's chorale "Jesu, Joy of Man's Desiring." Slides of Christ at first, then ads, domestic scenes, questions about love as, over the sacred music, we hear a man with a Spanish accent talk about the problem of raising his kids in the city: ". . . and I don't know how to combine both love and, at the same time, survival." A housewife then confesses that although her family has all the material advantages they'd ever dreamt of owning, her life is empty, devoid of any drive or meaning. Still with "Jesu" in the background, a quick succession of young people talk about love (or the lack of it), parents, listening, and caring. The movie projector spews forth a series of the mindless sort of television commercials.

Silence again, and the reader declares, "The people who walked in darkness have seen a great light . . ." (Isaiah 9:2-3). Three dancers appear in front of the screens, their features illuminated by the light from a color wheel. The

PEANUTS®　　　　By Charles M. Schulz

sound of a twelve string guitar introduces "Lord of the Dance." The slides are a combination of shots of the dancers (taken during a rehearsal), paintings from the life of Christ, scenes of celebration, and words of love, joy and hope. Along with the 16mm film of commercials in the center screen, an 8mm projector starts to unreel a film of the dancers; scenes of the life of Christ (photographed by placing large church school pictures on a music stand, setting the camera lens to telephoto and panning over the painting) were spliced in between the shots of the dancers. The effect is intriguing—we see the dancers before us and at various places on the screens as well.

After the dance interpretation a few of the lights are

turned on so that the congregation can join in reading Psalm 150. Then we hear a voice pleading "Teach me to dance, will you?" and Zorba's famous reply, "Did you say *dance?* Come on my boy!" The exuberant strains of "Zorba's Dance," recorded, with the dialogue, from the album, starts out slowly, soon picking up tempo and power. Slides of Zorba and Basil, posters, words, and scenes of celebration again flash by. The TV commercials go on and on, and the 8mm projector shows a newsreel depicting the joys and heartaches that have made the headlines. Zorba talks to Basil, suggesting that the one thing he lacks is a little "madness," the ability to cut the rope and let go. The slides show this scene from an encounter of the canine "Zorba" with his chief detractor. (See p. 75.)

PEANUTS ®   By Charles M. Schulz

But it is of no use, for Snoopy, like his human counter-part, must express himself, must affirm life by the means he knows best. Finally he convinces, not by rational argument but by contagious example, even Lucy, the "Pharisee of Pharisees," or should we say "Fussbudget of Fussbudgets"? (See p. 76.)

The music reaches a crescendo, stops and the speech choir reads another Norman Habel selection from *Interrobang*, "Sounds of the Eucharist":

... We wait for the sounds of God
and the sounds of the sacrament,
The breaking of bread
and the gushing of wine,
The pain of sorrow
and the pulse of hope ...

We hear the sounds in the distance,
the vibration of human lives,
The crackle of fear
and the murmur of distrust ...

In a moving manner the chorus, read antiphonally by two groups, sets the Eucharist in the midst of the pain and joy of our world, as was that first Supper.

"O taste and see that the Lord is good!" exhorted the Psalmist. We do just that. The sound of the Bread being broken by and for neighbors as it is passed around the semi-dark room. The smell and sound of God's good wine being poured and shared add to the sensory input.

Christ is present, His sacrifice is recalled. The Crucified is also the Resurrected One. But still his children, with whom he identifies, are crucified daily, often with little or nothing of the Easter promise of Resurrection to sustain them. Yet the Sacrament is our loyalty oath, our "sacramentum," to serve this Risen Christ by serving those whom he also claims as his brothers and sisters. And so the last visual interpretation, of the song "Let Me Come In." A combination of ghetto children's monologues and voices singing of their hopes and disillusionments, this powerful song from *The Me Nobody Knows* presents a stirring challenge to fulfill our oath to Christ.

Slides of children, words of love, alternating scenes of ghetto and suburban life, shots of refugees around the world, God's forgotten children. The television commercials have given way to public service spots. Joining the two sets of slides and the two films is a short filmstrip based on Matthew 25:12-31, entitled *Listen, Christian*.

The song and visuals reach a whirling climax in their plea for involvement. Then total silence for a moment. The machines are off. The choral speech group concludes with "Dreams For Celebration":

Leader: Today the Lord steps into the air once more to
        taste its color and feel its songs. He inhales
        the thoughts of children, the breath of yesterday,
        the fantasies of tomorrow, and he wonders whether
        his children are too old to celebrate their dreams.
Right: Let us spin him our dreams.
Left: Someday soon people will celebrate life every day ...[5]

And the dreams are spun out—visions of love and unending joy expressed in "wet and wild" ways. The congregation sings "We Are One in the Spirit," passes the Peace. The lights come all the way on. Expressions such as "Wow" or "What was it?" come from the congregation. Dancers, liturgists, technicians relax and answer questions from those wanting to stay around. The event is over but the experience lingers on.

---

[5] Norman Habel, *Interrobang.*

Gadgets,
Gimmicks
and
Grace

You can have the finest collection of slides, films and tapes ("software," according to media jargon), but you are nowhere without equipment ("hardware") to project them. This aspect of multimedia production is a major deterrent to many in the church. "We just can't afford all that expensive equipment!" "I don't know anything about projectors and cameras and stuff..."

Even if the educator is free of such hang-ups, he is often bewildered by the vast array of hardware and software available. In this chapter we will focus upon equipment, whereas in the last chapter we will be discussing in more detail films, records and the like.

A list of essential hardware would include, in order of importance:

1. Slide projector(s)
2. Record player
3. Tape recorder
4. An electric iron

5. Camera and close-up lenses
6. 16mm film projector
7. 8mm film projector
8. Movie camera
9. Film splicer and stop watch
10. Slide storage system
11. Flashlight
12. Light meter

The order may vary according to the kind of media production you are working on. I am assuming that you are just beginning to tiptoe into m-m production according to the method suggested in Chapters 2 and 4—from short, simple slide shows to two projector ones to multimedia. Thus for simple slide shows using lift-off slides only items No. 1 through 4 would be needed. The more elaborate your production, obviously the more equipment you will deem "essential." Eventually, you will want most of the following:

13. Dual 8 movie editor
14. Screens (esp. rear projection ones)
15. Slide sorter
16. Telephoto lens for camera
17. Copying stand
18. Slide duplicator
19. Overhead transparency projector
20. Opaque projector
21. Color wheel
22. Strobe light
23. Slide press

There are many books and publications designed to give you detailed technical information on such equipment (some will be listed in the following chapter and in the Bibliography). What follows are some comments from an amateur's viewpoint interested at this point only in such equipment as it relates to multimedia. Such information was gleaned largely from experience and in no wise makes me an expert on the subject. This should lend the reader some encouragement; few, if any of you could have started out with less knowledge and experience than myself. If I can learn (a process just barely begun), so can you.

You or your church may not own the necessary projectors and tape recorders. Don't let this stop you. Some possible ways of assembling the needed equipment:

1. By borrowing from—Members of the congregation
   —Local school or educational office
   —Scout office
   —Neighboring church
   —County Extension Agent or Soil District Office
   —Hospital—Training or P.R. Office
   —AV Department of a college
   —Regional Christian Ed. Office
2. Rent—Many camera and AV supply stores have this service.
3. Purchase—Jointly with one or more churches
   —Use church memorial funds
   —Youth, women's or men's group might be willing to take on a car wash or supper to raise funds
   —Start a campaign to collect enough trading stamps
   —Some pastors who receive extras such as gifts from weddings and funerals could use these for equipment.

Now for a closer look at the hardware:

SLIDE PROJECTOR These come in all shapes, sizes, and prices—filmstrip projector with an adapter, cartridge load type, autostack machines. Chances are that your church owns the first kind. If you plan to purchase a filmstrip projector, make sure it has a slide adapter; it's worth the extra money. Simple slide shows can easily be projected; our Junior Highs presented an excellent two-projector show on ecology with one of the boys deftly hand-feeding his slides into the filmstrip-with-adapter projector—and he easily kept up with the fast pace of the production.

Hopefully, you will have access to a cartridge/carousel type. (Make a survey of your congregation to find out what equipment your members have. Most pastors, even of small churches, would be very pleasantly surprised.) The performance of these vary as much as the price. When shopping around keep these questions in mind:

GADGETS, GIMMICKS AND GRACE

1. If you know someone who owns the machine, what do they say about it? (The AV department of a local school might be willing to give you some advice.)

2. Is it ruggedly constructed with a minimum of cheap plastic parts?

3. Can the slide cartridges be changed quickly in the dark? (And are the other controls easy to operate this way also?)

4. Can the bulb be changed quickly without special tools or without having to take apart the outer casing? How available and expensive are bulb replacements?

5. Does a local dealer offer service at his shop?

6. How quiet is the motor? (I'm assuming that you wouldn't even consider risking your slides in a machine without a fan!)

7. Is there a remote switch for both forward and reverse? Does the reverse take hold instantly? (On some makes a slide can be reversed only after the next slide is advanced.)

8. How many slides will the cartridges hold? (Some makes hold only 30 which is too few for serious m-m work. Kodak's 140-slide tray is too many, as anything other than the very thin cardboard slides, if they fit at all, tend to jam at crucial points. Trays holding 60, 80, and 100 slides work the best. The autostack projectors are nice for family slide viewing but not very practical for m-m work.)

9. How jam-proof is the slide feeding mechanism? (Of course, no machine is completely free of this problem, especially if your slides are bent or frayed.)

Optional, but not really vital, devices you may want are a zoom lens and a time device for automatically changing the slides.

If you have the capital or a rich uncle, the Kodak carousel models are excellent. They are reasonably quiet and sturdy, the carousel trays are easy to change in the dark and they have a lock-in ring to prevent your slides from spilling out. The professional media people I have met use Kodak's Ektagraphic line of projectors because of their dependability and relatively jam-proof mechanism. (As we warned before, though, do not try to use their 140-slide tray!) The chief drawback is probably the price (I don't own one yet myself), but in the long run they are well worth it.

For those with smaller budgets there are many other good projectors. I still use my $45 Argus 541 Projector, purchased eight years and hundreds of slide shows ago (and several trips to the repair shop I should add). It is not as sophisticated as the Kodak, one of the chief drawbacks being that when the reverse switch is triggered (located on the body of the machine rather than on the remote slide changer), the next slide is shown before the tray is reversed.

I also own a reel-type Airequipt machine. Purchased secondhand at about half the price of a comparable Kodak, the machine boasts of a remote forward-reverse and focus control, automatic focusing, and an automatic slide changing timer (from two to ten seconds). It's a good machine but with several problems: the forward-reverse switch must be handled with care lest it stick, causing a series of slides to zoom through at eye-popping rate; the reels are hard at first to change in the dark; the latter are easy to spill; the whole housing must be taken apart in order to change bulbs, a time consuming process. However, the reels do hold 100 slides, thus requiring fewer changes for your production.

For bargains, and there are many, check such publications as *Popular Photography* and *Modern Photography*. The difference in price between the mail order store and your local one, however, is but one consideration; you should note also the fact that a local dealer services what he sells and can be a good source of advice and help. In short, don't buy on impulse, but shop around carefully.

THE SOUND SYSTEM—TAPE RECORDERS AND RECORD PLAYERS There are too many brands available to be very specific as to which are best. As a general rule it is safe to say that any machine costing less than $50 (and some would set the figure much higher) should be put into the toy category. Definitely not for you. Check with a friend who knows something about electronics or the Consumers' Guide reports on tape recorders. If your budget forces you to choose between a reel-to-reel recorder and a cassette, pick the former. Only the more expensive AC-powered cassette machines will give you enough amplification for multimedia, and even then, the frequency range will probably not be as great as on a reel-type machine of comparable price. Buy or borrow the best you possibly can.

All good recorders will allow you to make tapes in two ways—with a microphone and with a patch cord. The mike will mainly be just for "live" voice recording. When dubbing something from a record always use the patch cord for the best fidelity. This allows you to record without picking up any room noise and with a minimum amount of distortion and static. Some record players will have a jack for the cord to plug into. For most phonographs the following fairly simple procedure (it has to be if I can do it) is required:

Unscrew the bottom or rear panel so that you can see the back of the speaker(s). Obviously a good quality mono machine is the easiest for this. You will need a patch cord with two alligator clips on one end and a finger plug for the input jack of the tape recorder. Find the two wires leading to the back of the speaker and attach a clip to each of the terminals or bare part of the wire leading in. Plug the other end of the cord into the proper jack of the tape recorder, and you're ready to make a direct recording of a record. If the playback is marred by static or muddiness, check the connections, especially the alligator clips, to make sure they are making good contact with the terminals or wires.

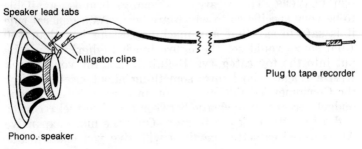

Speaker lead tabs

Alligator clips

Plug to tape recorder

Phono. speaker

GADGETS, GIMMICKS AND GRACE

If you have a stereo tape recorder, you can mix sound more easily, as was described in the account of *Signs along the Way*. Music can be recorded on one track, then you can go back and record voices or sound effects at the proper place on the second channel.

The sound should be recorded at such a level that it will not be distorted if played back at a louder volume level in a large room. Always check this out before each showing. Greater volume, when necessary, can be obtained by plugging your tape recorder into the amplifier of a PA system. When this is not possible, I have had good results from placing the PA mike near the speaker of the tape recorder. Often improvisation is the name of the game. Never be afraid to ask for help. What little I know of such matters has been learned from friends eager to be of help when asked.

Always remember that most groups are sophisticated graduates of thousands of hours of listening to films, TV, and stereo. Thus they will resent any marked lack of clarity in the sound, much more so than a poorly produced slide. So take care.

SLIDE CAMERA As has already been said in Chapter 3, you need not wait for an expensive camera before plunging into media work. The "Instamatic" variety will take good slides of well-lighted scenes around church and town. A three to four dollar portrait lens attachment will allow you to copy large pictures such as the covers of *Newsweek* or *Time* or the large kind found in so many Church School teachers' packets.

One word of caution: when taking a close-up picture, aim the camera slightly higher in order to get the actual area of the picture that you want. As you look through the viewfinder, you are seeing an area slightly higher than what the lens, and hence the film, sees. This difference, the distance from the center of the lens of the viewfinder to that of the camera lens, is called parallax. If you forget this, you may cut off the heads of your figures in the picture. (I did this while trying to copy a painting of Christ's

Resurrection!) A little experimentation will show you how much higher to sight.

Of course, if you plan to copy a large number of pictures from magazines and books, you will want a Single Lens Reflex camera. (I love to astound the uninitiated with the much used abbreviation "SLR"—a term I learned myself only very recently!) Not only is the parallax problem eliminated, but with adjustable lens and shutter settings, pictures can be made under a wide variety of lighting conditions.

The viewfinder of an SLR camera incorporates a system of mirrors that allows you to see through the lens of the camera. Thus "what you see is what you get." Many focus down to twelve or thirteen inches without additional attachments, enabling you to make close-ups of most magazine pictures. With special lenses or extension tubes extreme close-ups are possible. Telephoto lenses allow you to go to the other extreme of making candid shots of people far off.

A wide variety of films are available for such 35mm cameras. With "fast" film interior shots or night scenes can be made without the intrusion of a flash bulb. Stained glass windows, stage and chancel scenes, the action in a coffee house—all can be captured with the right film and the appropriate camera setting. A flood of books are available at your camera shop or library; these will give you the necessary technical information for producing good slides.

You probably have someone in your parish who owns an SLR camera and would be willing to help your group, either by serving as photographer or loaning his camera. This latter way was the means by which I first learned to use a reflex camera long before I was able to buy one.

Most people think that fine cameras are expensive. They are right, to an extent. You can spend hundreds of dollars for a camera loaded down with gadgets and gimmicks. A camera equipped with a through-the-lens meter system must be a joy to own since it insures that the camera's film exposure will always be right for the amount of light available. However, this is not absolutely necessary. A basic SLR camera can be bought from $50 to $75. Add a $15 to $20 separate light meter (instead of one costing $100 or $150 when built into the camera), and you are in the picture taking business, with practice and persistence, of course. If you are really on a tight budget, check the camera stores and the ads in the photography magazines for bargains in trade-in and reconditioned cameras.

16MM FILM PROJECTOR Of all projection equipment this is probably the most available. If yours is an old one sounding like a threshing machine, beware. It may do just that to the splicing in your film.

The Bell and Howell models are great if your church is planning to buy one. I have used a wide variety of projectors at workshops under all kinds of conditions and have found their newer models to be ideal for multimedia. Sometimes your film will jump out of alignment and start fluttering. This can be disastrous during a m-m production since it usually means having to stop the machine and open the gate. When this happens with B & H's, a very simple operation solves the problem: turn the direction control to reverse for half a second and then back to forward. The program is hardly interrupted.

The only drawback to this projector is the sound system. The speaker is built into the main unit rather than being in a separate unit, such as the lid. Although adequate for medium-sized rooms, an external speaker would help in larger situations. There is a jack for this purpose, so a hi-fi addicted friend could rig up one for you.

Major points to check out in any machine you may be considering:

1. How dependable is it? (This is allied pretty closely to price.)
2. How loud is the motor? Does it have a reverse?
3. How easily can you get in to change a bulb?
4. How clear is the sound system?

8MM PROJECTORS Like their big brothers, these come in

all shapes and sizes. Newer models can be had that will project both regular and Super 8mm, often with merely the flick of a switch. If you are just beginning filmmaking, by all means purchase Super 8 equipment. The picture is about forty percent larger and brighter than the older format.

Every media person probably has his favorite brand of projector. Most are good, and some are "gooder." I'm especially fond of the Keystone line as they seem to have a greater tolerance for film splices than the other models that I have used. My films are made up from quite a number of shorter clips. Often the film jumps out of the track in one of the more expensive models, but goes right through the Keystone projector.

Some of the newer projectors feature sprocketless drives, which should mean that your film will last much longer. The greatest amount of damage to a film is caused by the sprocket wheels chewing up the edge of the film. As in all things, let the buyer beware. Test any bargain with a reel of your own film before closing the deal.

MOVIE CAMERA Because of the high cost of camera, film and processing, we won't even discuss 16mm. Regular and Super 8 cameras can be found in every community. I have seen them in pawn shops for as little as $10. True, there were no fancy gadgets attached such as light meters and fade in/out devices, but the basics were there. Your best friend again is the advertising section of the photography magazines.

If you use the newreels or highlights from Hollywood films in your multimedia productions, sooner or later you will want to add your own footage to the reel. It may be scenes of your community and church. Perhaps a vignette acted out by your group. Or still shots of posters and magazine pictures. The possibilities are limited only by your imagination—and by the capabilities of your camera. Check into some of the books on films and filmmaking listed in the Bibliography for details.

Even the usual, limited camera found in many homes

affords many possibilities. In Chapter 5 a description was given of an interpretation of the folk-hymn "Lord of the Dance" in which both the two sets of slides and the 8mm film heighten the effect of the dancers. Both slides and movie were shot during a rehearsal from various angles: from the sides and from above and from behind the Cross which served as the focal point. The movie was made with a very inexpensive camera; a super deluxe model would have added nothing except the assurance, while the film was being processed, that the correct exposure had been made.

Beware, too, of filmmaking, for it can become a contagious disease causing itchy palms, drooling countenance, and extreme impatience, especially when you are scanning the back pages of photography magazines. Before buying, think carefully of what you want to accomplish with a camera. There are many special effects possible with good Super 8 cameras, but no one camera will have every feature, so choose one that, in line with what you can spend, will have the features that you will use the most. Some models use a through-the-lens viewing and metering system; lap dissolve and fade-in, fade-out control; zoom and even macro-zoom lens; different speeds; a sound-synchronizing system; acceptance of wide variety of films; time lapse device; and a host of other items. Only the most expensive camera costing over $350 would have the majority of these features, but a moderately priced camera costing between $100 and $200 would offer enough so that you could produce a film with intriguing effects. Thus you might have to choose between a camera able to film extreme close-ups or one that can give you professional "fades."

My own preference, given a limited budget, has been a camera with the through-the-lens meter and a macro-zoom lens. I am very pleased with Bolex's 155 Macro-Zoom. The metering system will save many, many feet of film from being overexposed or underexposed. With the macro-zoom lens a flower, postage stamp or small picture can be photographed so that it fills the screen. The possibilities of making kinestasis films are especially intriguing, as anyone who saw the two films on "The Smothers Brothers Hour" a few years ago will agree. Using magazine pictures, the filmmaker showed the events of 1968 in a little over three minutes, and by photographing pictures from history books, an interesting four-minute history of America. The technique, when you have the right kind of lens, is simple; you shoot a short series of exposures of still pictures, from four to eighteen or slightly more. Remembering that eighteen frames make one second, you can see that this results in a very fast-paced film, creating a multimedia effect in itself.[1]

FILM SPLICER AND STOP WATCH This may seem to be an unusual combination, but these two gadgets will allow you to edit your film so that each scene of the final product is exactly the length and in the correct sequence. Most film editors include a splicer; with this and splicing tape, you will be able to make good, lasting splices. Since the sprocket holes are different for Regular and Super 8 films, you will either need two different machines or the "Dual" type. Sixteen mm editors are very expensive, but this film can be spliced with a Regular 8 splicer since the sprocket holes of 16mm film are exactly twice as far apart as those of Regular 8.

You may be splicing together a series of TV commercials in their entirety or just short snatches of them. You might want to rearrange the segments of an 8mm newsreel or to add in your own footage. The editor-splicer will allow you to do this, and the stop watch will enable you to match the scene to the music or narrative.

FLASHLIGHT Basically for emergency use when something goes wrong, as it will sooner or later. It's even embarrassing when some eager beaver turns out the lights before you have all the slide controls in your hands and you're left fumbling around in the dark trying to locate

---

1 For more detailed information on kinestatic filmmaking see the book *The Creative Eye* and the Immedia 8 film *Image of Christ*.

them in the tangle of wires. With some slide projectors you may need one to see with in order to make smooth tray changes. Or you may want to check your script to see if everything is going along well. Other possible uses: as a mini-spot or with colored cellophane over the lens for special lighting effects.

SLIDE STORAGE SYSTEM A must when your collection grows beyond three or four hundred. There are three basic systems, each with its advantages:

1. IN CARTRIDGES. Ideal for storing those of a particular "show" which you will use over and over. It is also expensive since it ties up a number of trays and requires considerable storage space. A special directory or listing is required in order to find particular slides for other uses.

2. SLIDE STORAGE CASE. A small box or suitcase with separate slots for 100 to 500 slides, this is the least expensive method. The lid usually has a form for listing the slides. For quick access to them you will need to work out your own method of categorization, such as adults, children, crowds, celebration, faces, poverty, pollution, war, peace. Whatever topics enable you to find the right slide with a minimum amount of searching are best.

3. FILE FOLIO PAGES. Made of clear plastic, each page is divided into twenty slide-holding pockets. The pages are punched to fit into a three ring binder. This is a more expensive system at 35¢ a page, but it has the advantage of allowing you to see each slide as you flip through the folder. This makes the search for that just right slide for your next media presentation a lot less frustrating than having to take each slide out of a slot for examination, as you must with the other two systems. In the long run I have found that the time saved is well worth the extra expense.

Whichever system you choose, you must maintain and keep it in good order if it is to work for you. As you add to your collection, you will save a great amount of time if you do have a system.

ELECTRIC IRON Needed for ironing shut the frames of your homemade slides. You can find usable ones at a Salvation Army store for a dollar or so.

LIGHT METER Necessary for cameras that have adjustable lenses but no built-in metering system. You might be able to guess fairly accurately the correct exposure for daylight picture taking, but for low light situations you will be glad to have a meter handy. Their $15 to $30 cost is soon regained by the amount of film that you will save from being poorly exposed.

Other helpful gadgets and gimmicks:

SCREENS Completely unnecessary if you have a large expanse of blank wall. Most screens are far too small for m-m projection, tending to inhibit the arranging of the images. So inhibited are we by the confining edges of a screen that most hosts are surprised to find out, upon my arrival to present a m-m experience, that I won't use their screen. Take advantage of objects hanging on the wall such as a cross by projecting around or over it for special emphasis.

Rear screen projection is something you may want to try, especially for worship services wherein the noise of the projectors might be distracting. If you have priced the screens in an AV catalogue, you might think that you would need a grant from the Ford Foundation. Actually, you can make a pair of them six feet by six feet for about $10. In the housewares department of a large discount store look for a plain plastic shower curtain. It should be the milky white transluscent kind; when you hold your hand against the backside, you should just barely be able to see it.

Ask a carpenter friend to build a frame on which to hang and stretch the curtain:

A trustee at our church built two frames using two by fours split in half for the upright posts and a strip 2½" by 1" by 6½' for the two cross bars. The posts were notched so that the cross bars would fit in, and a hole drilled through the posts and bars to receive a large nail, which secured all three pieces together at the top, yet was easily removable for dismantling and storing the frame. The shower curtain will have holes in the top. Nails with large flat heads, driven into the cross bar at measured intervals hold the curtain up, and thumb tacks secure it

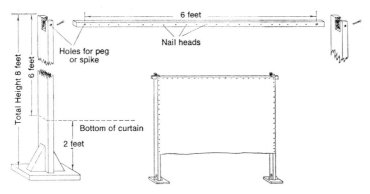

to the sides of the frame, also stretching the plastic for a smooth projection surface. Such a homemade rear screen system works beautifully at less than a tenth of the cost of a commercial one. Just don't forget to reverse your slides in their trays so that the audience on the other side of the screen can read the words. To reverse the image of a movie projector, show the film into a mirror set up so that it will reflect the reversed image onto the proper area of the screen; this will require some experimentation to get just the right angle.

A quick rundown on the remaining gadgets:

SLIDE SORTER This is a back-lighted screen with raised strips to hold the slides in four or five straight rows. Very convenient for selecting and arranging in the right order a series of slides for each segment of your production. You can buy one for a few dollars or use an old mimeoscope or a child's drawing scope.

TELEPHOTO LENS With an SLR camera this is great for obtaining candid shots of people in parks, streets, etc.

COPYING STAND The commercial ones vary widely in price. They provide a steady mount for your camera and usually have two lamps on goose necks—very handy for close-up copying. However, I have had good results from using a solid back music stand to hold the magazine in place and simply holding the camera myself; this makeshift method is good as long as there is sufficient light for shutter speeds of 1/30 of a second or faster.

SLIDE DUPLICATOR Available only for SLR cameras, this is attached in place of the regular lens. A slide is slipped into the holder, the device is pointed at a strong light source, and the picture made. This allows you to make duplicates of your best slides without having to send them away to a laboratory. All you send is the film from the camera itself.

OTHER PROJECTION SYSTEMS Just a reminder that other systems offer some advantages. Overhead transparency and opaque projectors are used in very few churches but are found in almost every school system. Strobe lights and color wheels can add just the right touch for certain scenes, especially when using dancers or actors.[2]

SLIDE PRESS I've only seen them in catalogues, but supposedly they are a faster, safer way of applying even heat to your slide frames. A real luxury when you consider the low price of an iron. You would have to make an unusually large number of slides to justify one.

As can be seen, media work can involve many gadgets and gimmicks. Just how many will depend on your imagination, ambition, and budget. Such work has its pitfalls, as we have warned, the chief one being the gadgets and gimmicks themselves. They are fascinating. They are fun, when they work and you have mastered them. They are also damnable when things go wrong. It is easy to become so caught up in the means that the message is forgotten.

The means can become ends in themselves. This is probably the most disastrous thing that can happen to a Christian educator. We all know someone who thinks that every event must become a T Group, a Simulation Game, Role Playing (Psychodrama nowadays) Event or whatever the current "in" technique is. Not every event will be suitable for projected visuals, so don't try to force one

---

2 The best book going into detail on such projectors is *Light: A Language of Celebration* by Kent Schneider and Sister Adelaide.

into situations calling for other techniques. There were exciting worship experiences long before Edison and Mc-Luhan. God's grace can still be communicated by non-electric means. Some would argue that in the final analysis it is only by person-to-person contact that such grace can be conveyed.

Finally, then, it is *you*, not your gadgets and gimmicks, that is the real conveyer of grace. Things *will* go wrong. Slides will jam. Bulbs will blow. A film will jump the track or break. A reader will blow a line. Maybe you'll even blow a fuse. If you are more involved with your gadgets and gimmicks than your message, this will show, and the experience really will be ruined. But if you yourself have experienced the message, if God's grace in Christ has freed you from your hang-ups, the situation need not be ruined at all. The Christian message *is* greater than the means. This, of course, is no excuse for sloppy preparation. A congregation today will spot this and reject the message. But if you have done your best to prepare, and something still goes wrong, be of good cheer. Your audience is usually sympathetic. And he who has "overcome the world," including that of technology—of gadgets and gimmicks—really is able to come through, both because of and in spite of your own efforts. I know. I have seen it happen time after time.

Moving

Experience

Filmmaking and Multimedia

A few ideas on filmmaking, touched on in Chapter 6, are worth exploring further. Many churches have found filmmaking an excellent way of involving a few individuals or a whole class in exploring Biblical values and themes. Nor do you need a Hollywood-size budget. Such home-produced films can be complete in themselves or used as a component of your multimedia productions. We won't go too much into the nuts and bolts of filmmaking in this short chapter. There are a number of excellent books on this, which are listed in the Bibliography. Consult these for information about camera shots, angles, equipment and the like.[1]

Don't let the equipment scare you off, either. Many leaders have been surprised when they have conducted an equipment survey of their church or class. People sometimes buy movie kits, use them for a while, and then put them away in a closet. Or you might discover a member whose hobby is filmmaking, yet who never thought it use-

[1] The May 1974 issue of the Methodist youth magazine *Face to Face* contains an excellent short introduction to the mechanics of filmmaking.

ful to the church! Check out secondhand and pawn shops and garage sales for used movie equipment at very cheap prices—this past year I picked up an old 16mm movie camera and a 16mm splicer-editor for $10 each. I've seen 8mm cameras for as little as $3. Along with a camera you will need a projector, a set of lights (unless you are using one of the newer "available light" cameras—by all means, if you are considering buying a new movie camera, consider this type), a film editor and a splicer. I am assuming that your camera has a built-in light meter; otherwise you will need a hand-held meter to keep from guessing about the amount of light present.

Let's assume that you have done your homework by rounding up the equipment, reading the books and manuals, perhaps even experimented with the camera. You know the difference between 8mm and Super 8mm and even which way to point the camera. Now what? You need an idea or theme, of course. (If you haven't any by now, go back and reread this book!) Sometimes ideas for a film will arise from your teaching materials; other times a special occasion to which you would like to give a different twist might suggest a film. Here are some for instances:

A senior high class had been studying the doctrine of creation in Genesis 1 and 2. They decided to make a film on God's world and what man is doing to it. Since they lived by the Ohio River, they focused in on this aspect of creation. The group shot footage of the river from rowboats, bridges, and the river bank. They captured scenes of beauty—of plants and animals—and of stark ugliness—of sewage and beercans and other such flotsam. Others of the group produced the sound track. They used parts of Genesis and a nature Psalm which they read over a song. Their choice of music was a stroke of genius; someone had brought a stack of records, among which was a song treating, not a river or ecology, but the love between a man and woman. However, when the film was shown in accompaniment with the love song, the application was evident to everyone—the "beloved" became the river. The combination was a short, effective statement of the class's concern for their part of God's creation.

My nine-year-old daughter once gathered six of her schoolmates and brothers to shoot a fairy tale which she had written. Her older brother served as cameraman and co-director. The same thing could be done with a children's class in the Church or Vacation Church School. The Bible is full of exciting stories, as Hollywood discovered long ago. Your film doesn't have to be filled with sex and gore and "a cast of thousands." There are many incidents and parables which call for unpretentious treatment. You can use simple costumes, or, because of the Bible's time-less quality, you could transfer the episode to the present day.

Unless you own one of the newer cameras capable of recording sound, you will not be able to use dialogue, but pantomine can be just as effective in getting the story across, as anyone who has seen such films as *Parable* will testify. Music or narration can be recorded on tape which is then played as the film is shown. You can also borrow a technique from the old time silent flicks by printing short statements or dialogue on poster board, filming them, and splicing each one in at the right spot during the editing process.

Several junior high youth in our congregation worked on a film that will form part of a multimedia production on Crucifixion and Resurrection. The group spent an entire session at Fellowship brainstorming on the theme. They divided a large sheet of newsprint into two sections, "Crucifixion" and "Resurrection," and listed whatever the terms suggested to them. "Death," "graveyard," "slums," "hospital," "war," "racism," "darkness," "loneliness," "old folks home," "winter," "pollution," "flowers," "spring," "sunrise," "children playing," "birds," "people helping others," "churches." These and a host of other words and phrases gave the group enough ideas to follow up and organize their project.

99

Two of the group shot an 8mm film of a number of the themes on the list, including a miniature Crucifixion scene. They hope to edit the film to match the sound track and slides put together by the other youth. The result should be a quick, kaleidoscopic treatment of the dual topic, linking that first Crucifixion and Resurrection to our own community.

Kids shouldn't have all the fun, however. Two friends produced a Super 8 film for a United Fund meeting of the employees at the chemical plant where they worked. They visited all of the United Fund agencies of the town plus some of the surrounding neighborhoods. The film which they obtained showed the needs of the community and the ways in which people were attempting to meet those needs. After considerable editing, the film was used in conjunction with slides and a tape recording for an exciting multimedia presentation.

A group wanting to study the mission needs of the church and community could launch a similar project. A list of people-serving agencies could easily be drawn up followed by an itinerary and schedule. The group would take along slide and movie cameras for filming the people and staff. Others of the group could interview some of the staff or people being served; the actual sounds of mission could be caught with cassette tape recorders. Still others of the group might roam through the neighborhood around the church or agency as they look for needs or just try to catch the flavor of the area; it's often surprising how different familiar surroundings can look when you have a camera in hand and a purpose in mind. From such a "Care" Trek a group could learn much about its community, its needs, and the ways in which people are trying to meet the needs. They might also uncover a need which no one is meeting. Through a multimedia, the group can share their experience and insights with others in the church and community.

Thus far we have explored filmmaking using live action. Another style that offers tremendous possibilities is called kinestasis filmmaking. For this you use a large number of still pictures, shooting only from one to eight frames a second. Thus your camera should have a single frame lever, though I have created several such films with my Bolex, which does *not* have such a control. If you were a fan of the old Smothers Brothers Show you might recall seeing the films *The World of '68* and *An American Time Capsule*. Both were short—about three minutes—yet the first covered all the important happenings of 1968 and the second took you on a *very* quick romp through American history. I've created a similar one racing through the major events of 2000 years of church history in five minutes; this forms the first part of a multimedia production on the mission of the Church.

The movie cameras you will probably use shoot film at 18 frames per second. Thus a four-frame shot will last slightly less than $\frac{1}{4}$ of a second, just barely long enough to register on your mind. By counting the number of frames, you can control the length of time that each picture stays on the screen. Sometimes you can race through a series of pictures, other times you can linger over one for two or three seconds, depending upon the mood you are trying to create. You can actually create a visual rhythm for your film in this way.

Your camera should also be capable of taking close-ups. For some you can buy close-up adapter lenses at a camera shop. Best of all are the macro-zoom cameras which allow you to come to within an inch or less of your subject. I have been able to focus in upon a small 3″ x 4″ picture in a book and move the camera across it, scanning the faces of the people. When you see it on the screen you would think that a large painting or photograph had been used.

The latter brings us to a second kind of technique used in kinestasis filmmaking. Not only can you create a quick succession of images flashing by, but by moving your camera you can create the illusion of motion. You can slowly pan across a picture or focus on details of it and jump from part to part. If your camera has a zoom, you can shoot the whole picture and zoom in on a section, or reverse the procedure.

For a Christmas multimedia I made the star of Bethlehem in a Nativity scene appear to twinkle by causing the camera to go in and out of focus a number of times. The donkey in the picture of Mary and Joseph traveling to Bethlehem appears to move—or at least his legs do. After a quick look at the trio, the camera comes in for a closeup of only the legs. I tilted the camera a number of times while shooting just six or eight frames. In the film itself, the legs appear to be moving back and forth.

For this same Christmas production I prepared two sets of slides of the same pictures that were used in the movie. Shown on either side of the film this makes for an excitingly different presentation of the ancient story of the Birth. Along with the usual Nativity type art I used many scenes from today, as well as a blend of the traditional and the contemporary Christmas music for the sound track. This could be quite a Christmas project for a church youth group.

A further possibility, as was touched on briefly in an earlier chapter, is to combine film that you shoot yourself with commercial films. The fine Castle Newsreel films have already been mentioned; for a multimedia on Martin Luther King, Jr., I combined such news footage from two or three different newsreels with the kinestasis film that I had made from several hundred photographs.

As part of a multimedia exploring the role of women I combined the following Super 8 films: a documentary on Marilyn Monroe, a vignette with my wife as the "star," a series of kinestasis scenes from magazines photographs, and part of a Miss America pageant shot from our color television set. Yes, it is possible to make movies of scenes from television. Not high quality, due to a "rolling effect" caused by the scanning pattern of the electron gun in the picture tube, but the quality will be good enough to use in a multimedia show.

For this you will need a Super 8mm camera that can take Kodak's Ektachrome 160 film. Regular film is not sensitive enough to pick up the relatively dim light of a TV set. Set your television controls at high contrast and fairly bright, then focus in on the screen, and shoot away. You can also do this, by the way, with your slide camera and high speed film. In both cases the detail should be good in the scene you are photographing, as some detail will be lost in the transfer, especially of crowd scenes.

Here are a few further hints for combining your films and slides. Shoot the same scene or picture with both your movie and slide camera. The appearance of the same image on two or more screens at the same time will be very impressive, giving a sort of visual underlining. You can also have the slides focus in on various details of the picture your movie is showing, or vice versa. Or one picture might appear in the movie with contrasting scenes in the slides, and then later the slides show the same picture.

In working with 8 or Super 8mm film you will definitely need a film viewer and splicer. This will enable you to see exactly the pictures you want to keep or cut out. Remember, the normal speed is 18 frames per second; you will want to keep this in mind when editing the film so as to match up with your sound track. You will never be able to match sight and sound perfectly, but you can synchronize them closely enough for multimedia purposes.

One warning on this process: be sure to use the same tape recorder for editing and matching film and tape as you plan to use when you show your production. The speeds of different tape recorders can vary by as much as ten seconds for a ten-minute show. You can't detect this with your ears, but it shows up when you use a cassette recorder for your editing and a reel-to-reel player for the actual show. Two of my senior highs didn't tell me that they were editing their film in this way, so that when they showed their film with a reel-to-reel tape, they found they were way out of sync—and had to reedit the film to match the reel sound track. Don't let this happen to you!

For splicing your film pieces together you can use either splicing tapes (*never* scotch tape!) or liquid cement. The latter is a little involved, so I prefer the tapes. They're fairly easy to use, as well as being quick.

None of the above information will equip you to rival Hollywood but hopefully it will stimulate you to try your hand at filmmaking. Your own films will enrich your multimedia by opening up horizons limited only by your imagination. I say imagination rather than budget since this is more crucial than money. By working as a group you can meet both needs—so go to it. Lights! Action! Roll 'em!

Resources

Where To Get What

Finally we discuss "software," the materials needed to make all the hardware come alive with sights and sounds. When possible the source, if not local, is given. The market is almost glutted with new materials, far too many for all to be included here. Of necessity this will be a selective listing, hopefully directing you to some of the basic materials. After that, you are on your own. Well, not entirely, for also discussed are several publications that will keep you posted on the latest materials and ideas. At least one of these will give you an opportunity to exchange your own brainchildren with others.

A. SLIDE MAKING SUPPLIES

1. Slide frames—camera store. Available in cardboard or plastic.
2. Contact paper—usually in "Household Goods" at local variety and department stores.
3. Sheets of colored plastic/acetate—office supply store.
4. Acetate inks—some art supply stores.

If you live in a small town where slide frames and such are hard to find, you should have Don Griggs's Catalogue. This teaching and media specialist offers all sorts of media supplies and books.
Write: Griggs Educational Service, 1033 Via Madrid, Livermore, CA 94550.

B. FILMS

1. 16MM

a. For outdated TV commercials check with your local TV station; call either the manager or the public affairs director. After a normal thirteen weeks of use the spots are ususally thrown out. Station policy will vary as to passing them on. Some managers will not allow any to be used but will destroy them. Some will give away any and all, particularly when they see what you are up to. Others will give away only public service spots. For best results work through a Radio-TV Committee of a Ministerial Alliance or Council of Churches, or team up with several nearby churches and ask one of the pastors to contact the public affairs director of the station. He might seem incredulous at first that you actually want old commercials, but once he understands that you will be using them in church education, chances are he will help you out.

b. There are also religious "spots" that you can buy for a reasonable price. Some especially good ones have been produced for television by the Presbyterians. These can be used by themselves or spliced in with other film footage.

1) *The Drug Game* and *The Long Trip* use the scare approach to drug education but are useful, I have found, spliced in with other films.

2) *Teach 'Em a Lesson* is a delightful sixty second Bonanza-style cartoon on the theme of forgiveness.

3) Best of all are the Jesus Spots; there are six, some thirty and some sixty seconds, showing episodes from the life of Christ—Jesus and the Rich Man, Jesus and the Rich Fool, The Woman Caught in Adultery, The Tribute Coin, the Call of Peter, and the Mocking of Christ. These are really well done; I've used them in a number of multimedia productions. Several would be great for a stewardship multimedia.

All the above are available (plus others—write for

the catalogue) from: Department of Public Media, United Presbyterian Church, Room 1920, 475 Riverside Drive, New York, NY 10027.

c. Other 16mm films—check your city or county library. Some systems offer free films. Many colleges and educational AV centers will loan films to church groups.

For short, provocative films for rent the best catalogue is: Mass Media Ministries, 2116 N. Charles St., Baltimore, MD 21218. Some specific films that you should know about:

Parable—beautiful, creative film. Great for using with slides depicting the last days of Christ. Most film libraries stock this.

It's about This Carpenter—another short, unusual no-dialogue film on Christ. Both films available from MMM.

Why Man Creates—a feast for the eyes and mind, this Academy Award winner is a must for groups wanting to turn on to creativity. Awesome and funny, it is itself a prime example of creativity. It can be rented for $25 from: Pyramid Films, Box 1048, Santa Monica, CA 90406.

Teleketics is a series of colorful, imaginatively produced films on the sacraments and other theological/sociological issues. Their film *Water and Spirit* is an especially beautiful probe of baptism, very suitable for multimedia use, and not too expensive to buy. For descriptive literature write: Teleketics, 1229 S. Santee Street, Los Angeles, CA 90015.

2. 8MM—of the hundreds of titles available, the "Castle News Headlines" may be the most useful. Produced in Regular and Super 8 format, this series highlights the major events of every year back to 1937—the great and infamous people, war, riots, etc. You can also buy many documentaries, excerpts from Hollywood features, cartoons and comedies, and most of the great vintage screen classics. For fascinating lists that include all the above and more write: Blackhawk Films, J51, Eastin-Phelam Bldg., Davenport, IA 52808; Niles Film Products, 1019

S. Michigan Street, South Bend, IN 46618. Both companies offer bargains in used 8 and 16mm films plus a wide selection of slides and equipment.

Immedia 8 is a great package if you can come up with $450. For this you recive a Technicolor 1000 Super 8 sound projector that is a marvel to use and six films and discussion booklets. My former parish joined with another church to purchase this and found the films adaptable for many situations. *Beatitudes* is a lovely probe of Jesus' words using Corita Kent's famous mural and film clips from the circus, political rallies and peace demonstrations; this film alone would cost almost $300 if bought in 16mm format. *The Gumball Man* is a delightful account of a disheveled street wanderer bringing gumballs to children. *Image of Christ* is a fast-paced kinestasis film based on the Matthew 25 passage "Lord, when did we see you ... ?" It's only five minutes long, but over 300 images of faces, people, TV films clips and an intriguing sound track challenge your ability to perceive. For a colorful sheet describing these and other films write to: Immedia 8, United Church Press, 1505 Race Street, Philadelphia, PA 19102.

C. MULTIMEDIA PRODUCTIONS

Perhaps you would like to see someone else's work before trying your hand at producing a media show. The best way to get a group excited about creating their own is to have them experience one. Or maybe you are caught short of time and simply do not have sixty or a hundred hours to spend. The following can help you:

Change uses three 16mm projectors to depict changes in ecology, medicine, technology and religion; the cost is $13. Write to: Division of Public Media, Room 1920, 475 Riverside Drive, New York, NY 10027.

Camelot Communications will send an attractive booklet describing their numerous productions for rent or purchase. Ranging from 3½ to 30 minutes, these cover various subjects and use from one slide projector to three.

Records, tapes, slides, and technical services are offered by writing: Camelot Communications, 3820 Park Avenue S., Minneapolis, MN 55407.

"Media Explorations At Large" (M.E.A.L.), according to Mass Media Newsletter, offers a traveling production one hour and fifteen minutes long called *Damn Everything but the Circus.* For rates and availability contact: The Rev. Bill Joyner, Director M.E.A.L., P.O. 224, Wilton, CT 06897.

"Visual Parables" are multimedia kits, some of which were described earlier, available for rental from the author. For a descriptive leaflet contact: Visual Parables, Bethel Presbyterian Church, 2999 Bethel Church Road, Bethel Park, PA 15102.

D. FILMSTRIPS

The quality of the thousands that are available vary widely. Only a few are listed here. For others see the excellent AV guide *Media for Christian Formation* listed in the Bibliography.

Modern Art and the Gospel—The best AV tool available for helping a group develop a prophetic eye or "theology of seeing." A number of modern works are explored and compared to the work of the Old Testament prophets or "seers." The record is excellent for adults, but perhaps too wordy for kids. The frames of such masters as Klee, Picasso, Mondrian, and Pollack are so good that you may do as several of us have done—buy a second copy and cut it up for slides. The relationship of faith and art, of the movements of our century and that of God are highlighted. Sold by denominational bookstores for about $15.

People, Emotions, and Riots—includes a b-w filmstrip, script and record with excerpts from speeches of civil rights leaders. Well worth $7.50 (from denominational bookstores).

Listen, Christian—a hard-hitting challenge to Christians to take seriously Matthew 25:31-46. Available for

$5 from Pflaum/Standard, 8121 Hamilton Avenue, Cincinnati, OH 45231.

How Do You See Black America?—no script, just pictures in color depicting the world of the black man in America. Forty frames, $6.50—denominational bookstores.

Christ in the Art of Africa, Christ in the Art of China Christ in the Art of India, Christ in the Art of Japan, Christ in the Art of the Phillipines. Check your denominational book or mission center. Prices range from $5 to $7. Each strip contains beautiful reproductions and a narrative record plus national music of the country. They can be ordered from Methodist Board of Missions Service Center, 475 Riverside Drive, New York, NY 10027.

Crescendo—seventy-six frames, traces Negro protest from colonial days to late 1960s. $10 with record, $7.50 without. Denominational AV or book center.

The Rev. Dr. Martin Luther King, Jr.—SVE filmstrip, forty-three frames with record, $8.50. Good b-w photos depict highlights of Dr. King's life—many good frames. SVE, 1345 Diversey Parkway, Chicago, IL 60614.

Vietnam: A People in Agony—shows Church World Service in action in wartorn land. CWS, 475 Riverside Drive, New York, NY 10027.

Teleketics, already mentioned, has produced some beautiful filmstrips, as has Alba House. You should have both catalogues. Write: Alba House Communications, Canfield, OH 44406.

E. SLIDES

1. *Discovery in Slides* is the most ambitious of all the tremendous goodies offered by Paulist Press. The $75 cost might seem high, but the 200 slides contained in the album are excellent. For a group just beginning in media work, the printed aids and suggestions are very helpful. Several exciting leaflets describing their many materials will be sent to you by Paulist Press, 400 Sette Drive,

Paramus, NJ 07652.

2. For good nature, travel, railroad and New Testament slides see the Blackhawk Films address in Section B-2.

3. Camelot Communications, listed in Section C, has several sets of slides for sale interestingly called "Zonks."

4. Many camera and department stores stock NASA and travel slides.

F. RECORDINGS

The raw material for sound collages has never been more plentiful or inexpensive. Many discount stores offer periodic record sales where unheralded gems can be discovered. I have purchased at three for $1 discs of Dick Gregory, Martin Luther King, Jr., Shelley Berman, and the Smothers Brothers. At such prices it is easy to build a "sound library" with little money. Many fine singing groups which never made it big have produced good albums, sometimes including their version of famous hits (there must be dozens of interpretations of the Beatles' "Eleanor Rigby," for instance) ; these are often dumped in the cheap sales bins.

Of course, you should own, or have access to (two good sources: public library and the youth of your church), the works of such artists as Simon and Garfunkel, the Beatles, John Denver, Dion, Johnny Cash, Joan Baez, Buffy St. Marie, Phil Ochs, Harry Chapin, Jackson Five, Pete Seeger, Bob Dylan, The Carpenters, Vanilla Fudge and a host of others laying bare the realities of our times through word and music.

Many Broadway show albums provide excellent material: *Godspell, Jesus Christ: Superstar, West Side Story, The Me Nobody Knows* (anyone wanting material on youth and the ghetto should have both the album and the book of this!), *Camelot, Man of LaMancha, Fiddler on the Roof,* and such film albums as *Zorba the Greek.*

A good resource for interpreting secular music is Abingdon's "Disco-Teach," a record and study guide package.

This is especially helpful for groups just beginning to turn on to the possibilities of religious meaning in pop music (or "Top Ten Theology"). See the Bibliography (the buck passing really does stop there!) for helpful books and for magazines which print the lyrics of current songs. Your teenagers probably have some of these magazines. They can save you much time in getting the correct words (especially for rock hits, the singers of which are not exactly noted for clarity of diction).

You can purchase sound effects records also. One such album has such goodies as a "Small," "Medium," and "Large War." For a useful book and record catalogue write: Publishers Central Bureau, 33-20 Hunters Point Avenue, Long Island City, New York, NY 11101. This and other such companies offer many unusual records, books and posters in their periodic catalogues.

A fascinating tape cassette of religious radio spots can be ordered for $4.50 from The Radio-TV Dept., Detroit Council of Churches, 2111 Woodward, 200 Palms Bldg., Detroit, MI 48201. A full sixty minutes of sound, the subjects include love, family life, peace, drugs, the famous Freeburg spots (including his second series on the "God is Dead" theme). Sections of the tape can provide excellent discussion starters or voice tracks for your m-m sound tape.

The Mennonites have come up with a tremendous resource—a tape cassette called *The Greatest Week in History*. It's a professionally produced "You Are There" series of radio broadcasts covering Holy Week, a broadcast for each day in fact. Along with coverage of the major events in Christ's life are a number of authentic touches such as traffic and accident reports. A real buy for $5.00 from: Mennonite Broadcasts, Inc., Harrisonburg, VA 22801.

Excellent religious music in a folk and rock vein should be in your own or your church's library. Listed below, with their sources, are several we have found very useful:

Keep the Rumor Going by Robert Edwin. "...God is

Alive," is the rest of the fine title song. Especially popular with our youth is his twelve-string guitar accompanied version of "Lord of the Dance." One of those "must" albums. A newer release with more of a rock tone is "With Joy."

Joy Is Like the Rain by the Medical Mission Sisters. This includes songs popular with children and adults such as "Zacchaeus," "It's a Long Road to Freedom," and "God Gives His People Strength" (and the title song, of course).

Ring Out Joy—good collection by Ed Summerlin, jazz musician.

Follow Me—a gorgeous collection of New Testament-based songs by John and Amanda Ylvisaker. His treatment of "Judas" will compare well with "Herod's Song" from *Superstar*.

For these and other beautiful albums contact: Avant Garde Records, 250 W. 57th Street, New York, NY 10019.

A company that has probably done more than any other to spread the use of folk hymns, through their *Hymnal for Young Christians*, is the Friends of the English Liturgy. Their Ray Repp albums are also essential for a well-rounded collection. Our own youth have used many of these in producing radio programs as well as media shows and worship services. A few of their many offerings:

Mass for Young Americans
Come Alive with Ray Repp
Allelu
Sing Praise! Sing Praise to God

The above four albums contain the widely known hymns "Allelu," "Sons of God," "Of My Hands," "All You People, Clap Your Hands," "Shout from the Highest Mountain," "Here We Are All Together"—and many more so suitable for worship experience.

Other good F.E.L. albums: *They'll Know We Are Christians by Our Love; Run, Come, See* (this contains many beautiful communion and children's songs) and *The Cold Cathedral.* Their address: F.E.L. Publications, Ltd., 1307

S. Wabash Avenue, Chicago, IL 60605.

Still another source of good records is the World Library of Sacred Music (WLSM). Of their many productions:

There'll Come a Day—Montfort Singers put new texts to familiar melodies (Bob Dylan's song "The Times, They Are A'Changing" is slightly rewritten to form a hymn of challenge).

Gonna Sing My Lord and *Hand in Hand* by Joe and Maleita Wise. Especially melodious and related to the Communion liturgy, peace, love and justice.

For their catalogue write: World Library of Sacred Music, 2145 Central Parkway, Cincinnati, OH 45214.

For an album that already includes several contemporary services and sound collages suitable for visual interpretations, get Kent Schneider's *Celebration For Modern Man*. A young jazz musician/theologian, Kent Schneider has been doing some exciting writing and producing at the Center for Contemporary Celebration. His hymnal, *Songs For Celebration*, is a beautiful feast for the eye and soul. Both hymnal and record can be ordered from: Center For Contemporary Celebration, P.O. Box 3024, West Lafayette, IN 47906.

For useful voice tracks, sounds of mission and music you should know about:

1. *New*—a "multimedia communications service presenting the sound, the feel, the look, the ideas of ecumenical mission." During its short existence this was my favorite "periodical." Each edition surveyed a specific issue via articles, pictures, posters, a record with songs, sounds of mission, etc., plus directions for use. A real pity it folded. Some back issues are available, listed in some issues of the magazine's successor *New World Outlook*, or write: World Horizons, Inc., Room 1268, 475 Riverside Drive, New York, NY 10027. Any available issues should be grabbed by media folk at the reasonable price of $1.25.

2. Other albums of religious music:

God's Trombones—Fred Waring's Pennsylvanians,

114

Decca.

Jesus Christ: Superstar—Decca; what more needs to be said about this?

Godspell—many of us rate this higher than *Superstar*.

Truth of Truths—Oak Records has brought out this two-record "rock opera" that starts with Creation and hits the high points of both Old and New Testaments. Highly recommended; portions of it are outstanding!

3. Two good albums that contain the sounds and the voices that made history in the sixties are:

Decade of the 60's—Yorkshire Records 27009 (2 records).

I Can Hear It Now/The Sixties—Columbia M3X 30353 (3 records).

Available in record stores, these should be "musts" for your media soundtrack resources library.

For budget-minded persons, we should mention such clubs as "The Record Club of America." This outfit offers some of the best bargains in rock, pop and classical music to be found anywhere. Their regular prices and periodic sales are well worth the lifetime membership fee of $5. They often feature bargain prints as well—such as a large copy of Picasso's *Guernica* for $3.98. Check out their ads in various literary and critical magazines. Or ask a friend who belongs; he will jump at the opportunity to earn two free records for recommending you, and you will receive three freebies of your choice for joining.

To find out what records are current and worth buying, you should be a reader of Mass Media Ministries Newsletter. All the best and latest folk-hymn albums, as well as those secular ones of interest to church folk, are analyzed and discussed.

Abingdon Press produces two series of tape cassettes that many people find helpful. RAP and SOS, created by Dennis Benson, are designed to help youth leaders teach in creative ways by using AV and people resources.

G. POSTERS

Not every component of mixed or multimedia need be

mediated through a projector. Posters can also be a vital part of your media experience. There is such a variety of beautiful ones available that you should be able to find just the right ones expressing the theme of your show or celebration. Posters can reinforce your message before and after the lights are turned out. Tape them around the edges of your screen area (if you're projecting on walls), on posts and pillars, doors and windows—wherever the combination of bright colors and message will catch people's attention.

Some mention has been made of the companies that offer prints and posters for sale. The major ones are:

1. Abbey Press, Saint Meinrad, Indiana 47577.
Their catalogue, a real feast for the eye and soul, contains fine art objects and hangings in addition to their bright posters. Those of you seeking new ways of expressing ancient theological truth will especially appreciate the latter, as their posters tend to have more of a Christian orientation than those offered by most other firms. Shoot slides of the posters which you plan to display around the room and the impact of the message or mood you are seeking to convey. An example: Many people have commented on the slide-poster which I have used with the song "I Am A Rock"; the logo for this reads: "People are lonely because they build walls rather than bridges."

2. American Bible Society, P.O. Box 5656, Grand Central Station, New York, NY 10017.
They offer brightly colored sets of "Love" and "Joy" posters at bargain prices. Great for celebrations.

3. Argus Communications, 7440 Natchez Avenue, Niles, IL 60648.
Their gorgeous catalogue in the past has been printed on slick paper, enabling us to "lift off" the pictures. Play fair with them, however (as with all such companies), and buy some of their stock. Such companies can continue to make beautiful items available only as long as church folk continue to pay for what they use.

4. Full Circle Associates, 426 East 119th Street, New York, NY 10035.
Their posters, some actually in the shape of circles, vividly capture the joy and anguish of urban life. The proceeds from the sales help support the work of Father Robert Fox and his associates in Spanish Harlem.

5. Pflaum/Standard, 8121 Hamilton Avenue, Cincinnati, OH 45231.
Along with some of the best media books available, this firm produces fine posters, many of them the photo type. Especially good is their striking series called "Listen Christian," a jarring probe of Matthew 25:31-46. There's an excellent filmstrip that goes with this also.

6. Sacred Design, 840 Colorado Avenue, S. Minneapolis, MN 55416.
Many striking prints, cards and art objects are offered by these folk. Theirs is another catalogue that you should have in your collection; it's the kind you never throw away.

H. TO KEEP UP WITH THE CURRENT

So many new resources—films, filmstrips, books, records, posters, etc.—are being marketed today that it is difficult to keep up with everything. The following resources will not only inform you of what's new but also provide both evaluation and information as to what is good.

1. *Mass Media Newsletter*—as already mentioned, both their film catalogue and the Newsletter are indispensable for media persons wanting to keep up. The address is 2116 N. Charles Street, Baltimore, MD 21218.

2. *Eye on the Arts*, monthly newsletter of St. Clements Film Assoc., 423 W. 46th Street, New York NY 10036. Good film and TV reviews, worship and film ideas, well done film discussion guides. Editor Stan Summers is very helpful in booking and suggesting films.

3. Life-Time Cassette, P.O. Box 871, Nashville, TN

37202. Bill Wolfe interviews Top 40 stars, analyzes music and youth movements, includes cuts from new albums. Good resource; several churches could afford the cost by going together. He also publishes an excellent newsletter called *Music and the Young* which keeps you up with current music. He often suggests specific songs as good media soundtrack material and tells you where you can get them.

4. *Media and Methods,* P.O. Box 8698, Phildelphia, PA 19101. A monthly general educator's magazine exploring AV's. Some of the best articles on filmmaking and study, use of TV. Also good for keeping current on new hardware and AV's.

5. *Super 8 Filmmaker,* 10 Pelham Parkway, Pelham Manor, NY 10803 (bimonthly). Lots of good ideas on filmmaking in every issue as well as good reviews of new equipment.

6. To keep current *and* share your ideas: *Probe,* 220 Grant Street, Pittsburgh, PA 15219. Ten issues a year ($5). This is crammed with brief descriptions of liturgies, papers describing educational-worship events, books, records, posters, people available. It's hard to imagine the "emerging church" without *Probe.*

7. *Recycle,* P.O. Box 12811, Pittsburgh, PA 15241. Nine times a year, $6.50. Dennis Benson's "theology of junk" in the flesh, this gem is filled with ideas from the editor and readers (mainly *Probe* folk) on how to have a ball ministering in our throwaway culture. Dennis and Marilyn also publish *Scan,* a newsletter containing reviews of all sorts of books, films, games and materials, much of it of interest to media folk.

We live in an age flooded with good materials. Some of it is intended for Christian enablers. Often the most useful, as Corita Kent has shown us, were not so intended. But those with "eyes that see and ears that hear," and we hope that's *you,* will select from all the goodies and junk that which can be the bearer of the divine. To discover for yourself and to help others also to see the mysterious Presence in the midst of the ordinary is the most exciting work-play in the world. It's your playful task to enable young and old to:

... send up ballons in church
Turn tired old cathedrals into cafeterias
Paint gravestones as bright as the sun ...
Bounce through the mountains on beach balls
Write their Christian names in the sunset
Become as free as that man called Jesus Christ ...
Yes, someday soon people will live like that,
But we plan to start right now
Right now, Lord. Right now.
Amen, Lord, right now.[1]

Right on! Multimedia will not solve all the problems of church and world—it might even create a few more for you at times. But hopefully this book has shown you some of the possibilities for seeing and hearing in new ways. So "plan to start right now, Right now, Lord. Right now. Amen, Lord, right now!"

---

1 "Dreams For Celebration," *Interrobang*.

Annotated Bibliography

The following books and articles have helped me over the years in developing a theology of seeing. They are offered for the reader who would like to follow the probings of the various chapters to see where they might lead.

I TOWARD A THEOLOGY OF THE ARTS AND MEDIA

Abbey, M. *Man, Media and Message.* New York: Friendship Press, 1969.

Benson, Dennis. *The Now Generation.* Richmond: John Knox, 1969.
Should be put into the hands of every adult working with youth; approaches youth culture through its music.

Berger, Peter L. *The Precarious Vision.* Garden City: Doubleday and Co., 1961.
A fascinating book on the "roles" we assume, willingly and unwillingly; contains good discussion of the tragic and the comic aspects of life.

Bloy, Myron B., ed. *Multimedia Worship.* New York: Seabury Press, 1969.
Not much "practical" information, but an interesting collection of reactions of various theologians and artists to a m-m worship service.

Cook, John W., ed. *The Arts in the Communication of Faith.* Nashville: The Graded Press, 1969.
A good bargain price collection of short articles, many of them by artists. There is also a Teacher's Book available.

Cox, Harvey. *The Feast of Fools.* Cambridge: Harvard University Press, 1969.
Fascinating and stimulating book by one who has been in the vanguard of those probing the place of festivity in life.

————. *The Secular City.* New York: MacMillan, 1965.

Eller, Vernard. *The MAD Morality.* Nashville: Abingdon Press, 1970.
Not a media book, but a good exploration of the Ten Commandments filtered through *Mad* magazine. Several sections offer good ideas for provocative slide shows.

Engstrom, W. A. *Multimedia in the Church: A Beginner's Guide for Putting It All Together*. Richmond: John Knox, 1973.
> Has lots of good ideas; geared to church with plenty of equipment.

Eversole, Finley, ed. *Faith and the Contemporary Arts*. Nashville: Abingdon Press, 1962.
> A good, solid collection of lengthy articles on most of the arts.

Hazelton, Roger. *A Theological Approach to Art*. Nashville: Abingdon, 1967.
> A *must* for serious thinking on the subject.

Kent, Sister Mary Corita, Cox, Harvey and Eisenstein, Samuel A. *Sister Corita*. Philadelphia: Pilgrim Press, 1968.
> Beautiful and expensive—by all means get it.

Marsh, Spencer. *God, Man and Archie Bunker*. New York: Harper and Row, 1975.
> Complete with selections from scripts and stills of the characters, this is a good example of "media theology." For me a painful book in that after my *Christian Century* article about Edith Bunker I had hoped to write such a book.

McElvaney, William K. *The Saving Possibility*. Nashville: Abingdon Press, 1971.
> A delightful chapter on "celebration is..." alone is worth the price of this paperback.

McLelland, Joseph C. *The Clown and the Crocodile*. Richmond: John Knox, 1970.
> Not as widely known as Cox's *Feast of Fools* but for my money just as good; contains an excellent probe of the Bible in relation to the comic and the tragic.

Mueller, Willam R. *The Prophetic Voice in Modern Literature*. New York: Association Press, 1959.

Short, Robert. *The Gospel According to Peanuts*. Richmond: John Knox, 1964.
> A "must" book.

————. *The Parables of Peanuts*. New York: Harper and Row, 1968.
> Both delightful and scholarly—a rare combination. One of the best works on theology and the arts.

Schreivogel, Paul. *The World of Youth, The World of Art*. Minneapolis: Augsburg Publishing House, 1968.
> A survey of religion and the arts and a source book of ideas —good for leaders and groups just beginning to explore the arts.

Smith, J. C. *Good News, Anyone?* New York: Friendship Press, 1970.
> Good for groups beginning to probe the media and Christianity.

Tillich, Paul. *Theology of Culture.* Edited by Robert C. Kimball. New York: Oxford University Press, 1959.
> Probably everyone writing in the area of religion and the arts is indebted in some way to Tillich's work. His *Dynamics of Faith* and *The Religious Situation* also bear on the subject.

Vos, Nelvin. *For God's Sake Laugh!* Richmond: John Knox, 1967.
> Short but helpful.

Whittle, Donald. *Christianity and the Arts.* Philadelphia: Fortress Press, 1967.
> Nine short chapters cover virtually all of the arts of interest to the church educator.

Wilder, Amos N. *Theology and Modern Literature.* Cambridge, Mass.: Harvard University Press, 1958.
> Old perhaps but still good.

II LEARNING, THEORIES AND STUFF

Allen, Don. *The Electric Humanities.* Dayton, Ohio: Pflaum, 1971.
> A fascinating analysis of the electronic media and their impact upon us. If you have trouble understanding Marshall McLuhan, this is for you.

Babin, Pierre, ed. *The Audio Visual Man.* Dayton: Pflaum, 1970.
> A well illsutrated collection of essays on media and teaching. Good practical information, especially on interpreting and using pictures and slides.

Benson, Dennis. *Electric Love.* Richmond: John Knox Press, 1973.
> This is a very good combination of practical media ideas and personal reflections and theologizing.

————. *Let It Run.* Richmond: John Knox Press, 1971.

————. *Recycle Catalogue.* Nashville: Abingdon Press, 1975.
> A fantastic fun-filled feast of ideas (700 of them!) for recycling objects and ideas for the church. A good index helps locate ideas, church seasons, etc.

Coleman, Lyman. "Serendipity Books." Scottsdale, Pa.: Halfway House.
> Beautiful in format, these provide instructions and ideas for small group study and multimedia celebrations.

Consumers Guide—Photographic Equipment Test Reports. Skokie, Illinois: Consumers Guide Magazine, published annually.
> A *must* for anyone ready to purchase a new camera (still or movie) or 8mm and slide projectors.

Dalglish, William A. *Media for Christian Formation.* Dayton: Pflaum, 1969.

————. *Media Two,* 1970.
> Two *extremely* helpful volumes that review and analyze hundreds of films, filmstrips, posters and records.

Full Circle Play Book. Collegeville, Minn.: Liturgical Press, 1970.
Intriguing suggestions for using the colorful Full Circle posters.

Griggs, Donald C. Griggs Educational Services, Box 362, Livermore, California 94550.
Don is a media free-lancer whose catalogue should be in your hands; lots of goodies and ideas here.

Holt, John. *How Children Learn.* New York: Pitman Publishing Corp., 1969.
All of Holt's works are intriguing to those involved in teaching and learning.

Jensen, Andrew and Jensen, Mary. *Audiovisual Idea Book for Churches.* Minneapolis: Augsburg Publishing House, 1974.

Kuhns, William. *The Information Explosion.* New York: Thomas Nelson, Inc., 1971.
Good survey of electronic media and of Marshall McLuhan's ideas.

Leonard, George B. *Education and Ecstasy.* New York: Dell Publishing Company, 1969.
Opens up all kinds of probes concerning education.

Little, Sara. *Learning Together in the Christian Fellowship.* Richmond: John Knox Press, 1962.

McGuirk, Donn. *Better Media for Less Money.* The Arizona Experiment, 1972. 6947 E. MacDonald Drive, Scottsdale, AZ 85253.
These people are really into the education of teachers. Their materials, such as this one, are very helpful for church educators.

McLuhan, Marshall. *Culture is our Business.* New York: Ballantine Books, 1970.

————. *The Medium is the Message.* New York: Bantam Books, 1967.

————. *Understanding Media.* New York: McGraw-Hill, 1964.
Not easy going but certainly mind-expanding.

Schneider, Kent and Sister Adelaide. *Light: A Language of Celebration.* Center for Contemporary Celebration, 320 North Street, West Lafayette, IN 47901.
A *basic* resource for anyone wanting to really explore projectors (especially overheads) and light in liturgy.

Schutz, William C. *Joy: Expanding Human Awareness.* New York: Grove Press, 1967.
Good introduction to the human awareness movement.

Slusser, Gerald H. *A Dynamic Approach to Church Education.* Philadelphia: Geneva Press, 1968.
One of the few works on the subject that I did not want to lay down.

Tobey, Kathrene. *Learning and Teaching through the Senses.*

Philadelphia: Westminster Press, 1970.
>Contains a number of good ideas worth trying out.

Unique Lighting Handbook. Edmund Scientific Corp., Barrington, NJ 08007.
>A gold mine of ideas for light shows. Ask for their catalogue also (among the goodies—large weather balloons suitable for "screens").

Valdes, John and Crow, Jeanne. *The Media Works.* Dayton: Pflaum/ Standard, 1973.
>A lavishly illustrated, very creative survey of mass media. Contains lots of ideas for projects and discussion.

Woods, Richard. *The Media Maze.* Dayton: Pflaum, 1969.
>Includes one of the best simplified explanations of Marshall McLuhan's ideas and of mass media. Good for senior high through adult level; low priced.

III MUSIC—Getting Beyond the Beat

Eisen, J. *The Age of Rock.* New York: Random House, 1966.
>Very helpful for new and old rock fans.

Goldstein, R. ed. *The Poetry of Rock.* New York: Bantam Books, 1969.
>Good collection of rock lyrics.

Heyer, R. *Discovery in Song,* I and II. Paramus, N. J.: Paulist Press, 1969 and 1971.
>The whole Discovery series is excellent, this one proving especially popular with our youth. The words of various songs are explored through pictures and questions.

Savary, L. *Popular Song and Youth Today.* New York: Association Press, 1971.
>Very well done.

IV FILMS—From Reel to Real and Back

Audio-Visual Resource Guide, 9th Edition. New York: Friendship Press, 1972.
>A fine tool for locating and reviewing AV's pertinent to the church. Contains many helpful AV hints.

Bolex Reporter c/o Paillard Inc., 1900 Lower Road, Linden, NJ 07036.
>For those desiring to explore filmmaking techniques and ideas, these folk offer all fourteen back issues of this exciting magazine in a package deal. Write for details. Lots of help here.

Dalglish, William et al. *Media III.* Dayton: Pflaum/Standard, 1973.
>This is the third in a series of books reviewing films, film-

strips, posters, records. An *invaluable* set—should be in every media library.

Editors of Eastman Kodak. *How to Make Good Home Movies.* Rochester, New York: Eastman Kodak, various editions.
> Good, well illustrated handbook.

Gaskill, A. C. *How to Shoot a Movie Story.* New York: Morgan and Morgan, 1960.

Heyer, R. *Discovery in Film.* Paramus, N.J.: Paulist Press, 1967.
> Developed for the high school Discovery curriculum, this is a detailed examination of numerous short films.

Jones, G. W. *Sunday Night at the Movies.* Richmond: John Knox Press, 1967.
> Another "must" book; makes going to the movies twice as much fun.

Kuhns, William and Stanley, Robert. *Exploring the Film.* Dayton: Pflaum, 1968.
> Created for a film study course, this book is delightful to the eye and effective in opening up the language of the film. Good hints on filmmaking comprise the last chapter.

Rynew, Arden. *Filmmaking for Children.* Dayton: Pflaum/Standard, 1971.
> *Very* helpful for adults, no matter what age you are working with; perhaps the most practical book for beginning filmmakers.

Savary, L. *Contemporary Film and the New Generation.* New York: Association Press, 1971.
> Good study of the secular film.

John, David A. *Film: The Creative Eye.* Dayton: Pflaum, 1970.
> *Very* helpful for the filmmaker, this examines several famous films and includes comments from their creators as to how they did it.

Sullivan, Sister Bede. *Movies: Universal Language.* Notre Dame, Indiana: Fides, 1967.

Summers, Stanford. *Secular Films and the Church's Ministry.* New York: Seabury Press, 1969.
> A good short book by the long time critic and editor of "Eye on the Arts," the newsletter of The St. Clements Film Association.

V NEW WAYS OF CALLING UPON THE LORD

Abel, Paul and Van den Heuvel, A. H. *Risk: New Hymns for a New Day.* Geneva, Switzerland, obtainable at denominational bookstores: World Council of Churches, Vol. II, No. 3, 1966.

Adelaide, Sister. *Banners and Such.* West Lafayette, Ind.: Center for Contemporary Celebration, 1971.
> A fine book for all interested in banner-making.

Aherns, Jr., Herman, ed. *Tune In.* Philadelphia: Pilgrim Press, 1968.
    Good collection of photos, prayers and meditations. A favorite with our youth.
Bash, Ewald and Ylvisaker, John. *Songs for Today.* Minneapolis: Youth Department, American Lutheran Church, 1964.
Bimler, Richard. *Pray, Praise and Hooray.* St. Louis: Concordia, 1972.
    Colorful and joyful collection of prayers and poems.
Boyd, Malcolm. *Are You Running with Me, Jesus?* New York: Holt, Rinehart and Winston, 1965.
————. *Malcolm Boyd's Book of Days.* Greenwich: Fawcett World Library, 1969.
————. *Free to Live, Free to Die.* New York: Signet Books, 1968.
Brandt, Leslie F. *Good Lord, Where Are You?* St. Louis: Concordia, 1967.
    Good collection of prayers based on the Psalms.
Burke, Carl. *God Is for Real, Man.* New York: Association Press, 1966.
————. *God Is Beautiful, Man.* New York: Association Press, 1969.
————. *Treat Me Cool, Lord.* New York: Association Press, 1968.
Firnhaber, R. Paul. *Hymns for Now.* Chicago: Workers Quarterly, 1967.
    Available from The Board of Youth Ministry, The Lutheran Church—Missouri Synod, 210 N. Broadway, St. Louis, MO 63102.
————. *Hymns for Now II.* St. Louis, 1969. Also available from The Board of Youth Ministry.
F. E. L. *Hymnal for Young Christians* Vol. II. Chicago: F. E. L. Publications, Ltd., 1970.
Habel, Norman C. *Interrobang.* Philadelphia: Fortress Press, 1969.
————. *For Mature Adults Only.* Philadelphia: Fortress Press, 1969.
————. *Hi! Have a Nice Day.* Philadelphia: Fortress Press, 1972.
————. *Are You Joking, Jeremiah?* St. Louis: Concordia, 1967.
    These are great—highly useful for liturgies.
Haas, James E. *Praise the Lord.* New York: Morehouse-Barlow Co., 1974.
Haven, Robert Marshall. *Look at Us, Lord.* Nashville, Abingdon Press: 1969.
    Beautiful prayers and format, photographs. Pointed, conversational style.
Janssen, L. and Ryder, M. *Electric Liturgies.* American Baptist Church, Valley Forge, PA 19481.
    Quite a packet with four slides, balloons and an assortment of essays, liturgies and songs to make worship an electric ex-

perience.
Mead, Loren B., ed. *Celebrations of Life.* New York: Seabury Press, 1974.
    A delightful collection of short essays and liturgies growing out of the life of St. Stephen and the Incarnation Episcopal Church in Washington, D.C. A beautiful book to the eye— full of usable ideas for making liturgy "the work of the people."
Ortmayer, Roger, ed. *Sing and Pray and Shout Hurray!* New York: Friendship Press, 1974.
    A stimulating collection of liturgies and ideas by a pioneer in creative worship.
Pottebaum, G. A. and Winkel, J. *1029 Private Prayers for Worldly Christians.* Dayton: Pflaum, 1968.
    A "multimedia prayerbook." Glorious color and black and white photos. Book literally divided into three sections— horizontally!
Raines, Robert A., ed. *Creative Brooding.* New York: Macmillan Co., 1968.
    A well-chosen anthology of literary readings well suited for public and private worship.
Randolph, David J., ed. *Ventures in Worship, I, II, III.* Nashville: Abingdon Press.
    Good collection of worship resources—liturgies, prayers, etc. *Especially* good is the long essay in volume III: "Worship: Package or Probe?"
Rivers, Clarence Joseph. *Celebration.* New York: Herder and Herder, 1969.
    Beautiful, colorful, fun.
Rumpf, Oscar J. *Cries from the Hurting Edges of the World.* Richmond: John Knox, 1970.
    Good selection of choric readings dealing with love, ministry, population, hunger and other issues.
Schlegel, Ronald J. *Balloons, Anchors and Grappling Hooks.* St. Louis: Resources for Youth Ministry, Missouri Synod, Lutheran Church, 1971.
    An exciting collection of songs, liturgies and prayers guaranteed to enliven worship. These folk have since produced several other resources on creative worship well worth having.
Schneider, Kent. *Songs For Celebration.* Chicago: Center for Contemporary Celebration, 1969.
Strathdee, Jim and Stringer, Nelson, eds. *New Wine: Songs for Celebration.* Los Angeles: Board of Education of the Southern California-Arizona Conference of the United Methodist Church, 1969.
Ward, Hiley H. *Rock 2000.* Nashville: Abingdon Press, 1969.

Fascinating McLuhanesque format; deals with problems of the next thirty years—and a Christian's response. Included are photos, cartoons, art and brief notable quotes.

White, James F. *New Forms of Worship*. Nashville: Abingdon Press, 1973.

Wolfe, Betty. *The Banner Book*. New York: Morehouse-Barlow Co., 1974.

A *beautiful* exploration of creating and using banners!

VI SHORT AND SWEET—Magazine Articles

Burian, Jarka M. "Multimedia: The Scenic World of Joseph Svoboda." *Saturday Review of Literature*, August 28, 1971, pp. 35-36.

Carter, Nancy. "Mixed Media in the Church: We're Learning." *Church in Metropolis*, April, 1970, n.p.

One of the first and perhaps only "how to" articles. Well worth having, it was reprinted in *Colloquy* Magazine.

Face to Face. An outstandingly colorful youth magazine; if you're not Methodist, check with your neighboring Methodist parish about these back issues:

February, 1969—good article on Corita Kent

Setember, 1969—whole issue devoted to the film; best short articles I know of on this medium,

December, 1969—entire issue a delight, devoted to Christianity and the arts.

Kappler, Frank. "Film Revolution at Expo 67." *Life*, July 14, 1967, pp. 20-28.

Lots of beautiful pictures.

McLuhan, Marshall. "Playboy Interview." *Playboy*, December, 1968, p. 53.

McNulty, Edward. "Creating Your Own Multimedia Production." *Group Magazine*, October 1975, pp. 12-15. Available from: Box 481, Loveland, CO 80537.

Multimedia in a nutshell. This author at least tries hard—not bad for a beginner.

Randen, Larry C. "Electric Art Media." *Religious Education*, March/April 1973, pp. 251-252.

Larry, a pioneer in multimedia, has written many articles on the subject and develops media shows for national meetings.

Rigg, Margaret. "Sister Mary Corita i.h.m." *Motive*, December 1965, pp. 21-37.

A beautifully illustrated article.

Short, Garrett. "An Expert at Enthusiasm." *Spectrum*, November/December 1969, pp. 11-13.

Good reviews of films about Corita Kent and where to obtain them. (Other articles on graffiti and a Christmas celebration make this a valuable issue for media folk. This is a magazine every church should subscribe to.)

For the words of current songs the following magazines, obtainable at the magazine counters of drug and dime stores, are very helpful:

Best Songs
Song Hits Magazine
Hit Parader